New and Collected Poems

Leo Connellan

New and Collected Poems

PARAGON HOUSE
New York

This poetry has always been for
my wife, Nancy, and for my daughter, Amy

First edition, 1989

Published in the United States by

Paragon House
90 Fifth Avenue
New York, NY 10011

Copyright © 1989 by Leo Connellan

All rights reserved. No part of this book may be reproduced, in any form, without written permission from the publishers, unless by a reviewer who wishes to quote brief passages.

Manufactured in the United States of America

Library of Congress Cataloging-in-Publication Data

Connellan, Leo.
   [Works. 1989]
   New and collected poems / Leo Connellan.
     p. cm.
   Includes index.
   ISBN 1-55778-134-6
1-55778-162-1 (pbk.)
    I. Title
PS3553.054N47   1989
811'.54—dc19   88-22683
                                                              CIP

Contents

Grateful Acknowledgments ... xi
Preface ... xv

Death in Lobster Land ... 1
    Wawenock ... 3
    Sea Gulls Wait ... 4
    Origins ... 8
    Penobscot Raccoons ... 10
    Fair Warning ... 14
    In Lobster Night ... 15
    Scott Huff ... 20
    By the Blue Sea ... 21
    Edwin Coombs ... 30
    A Witness ... 44
    Amelia, Mrs. Brooks of My Old Childhood ... 45
    Garbage Truck ... 54
    In Maine We Own Our Sea ... 55
    Blueberry Boy ... 56
    From Five Islands Maine Rocks ... 57
    Hydrogen Now ... 58
    Lament for the Jews at Munich ... 59
    The End of the World ... 62

Another Poet in New York ... 63
    Lament for Federico Garcia Lorca ... 65
    Conscious ... 68
    Mommy's Hubby ... 69
    The Moon Now Flushed ... 71
    The Whole Thing About Jedge's House ... 78
    Staten Island Ferry ... 80
    Helpless, We Go Into This Ground, Helpless ... 83

Violent Dying	86
Autumn	91
Crossing America	93
Massachusetts Poems	117
Meeting Richard Wilbur	119
Boston	120
Visiting Emily Dickinson's Grave	122
What Can I Leave for You to Feel of Me	123
Four Short Poems	125
Through the World the Little Worm Forever	127
Boxing	128
The Assassin	129
Schwartz, in Three Words, Delmore, You Said "Keep Your Head"	130
New and Uncollected Poems	131
With Eberhart at Occom	133
York, Maine	134
Pulling Oar	136
Ode to Karl Shapiro	138
Oscar Wilde Lament	141
Motel	143
To War Dead	148
The Treachery of Flame	149
Winter	150
The Shadow of a Leaf	151
The Gunman and Other Poems	161
This Is a Stickup	163
On the Eve of My Becoming a Father	164
As an Apple Has Iron	165
Mundelein on the Michigan	166
Of the Betrayed	167

Penobscot Poems 169
    Lobster Claw 171
    Tell Her That I Fell 181
    Dark Horses Rushing 183
    Watching Jim Shoulders 184
    Shadows 185
    Closed Wake 186
    A Hen Crossing a Road 187
    Old Gravestones 188
    Old Orchard Beach Maine Burned Down 189
    Out Jim Moore's Window 192

The Clear Blue Lobster-Water Country 193
    Book I: Coming to Cummington to Take Kelly 195
    Book II: Shatterhouse 228
    Book III: The Clear Blue Lobster-Water Country 268

Earliest Poems: Poetic Thoughts, 1944 319
    Someday I'll Be Dead 321
    The Leaf 322

Grateful Acknowledgments

To Harcourt Brace Jovanovich for allowing me to include my trilogy "The Clear Blue Lobster-Water Country" in this *New and First Collected Poems*, specifically to Mr. William Jovanovich and to my editors, John E. Woods and John Radziewicz, gratitude for giving my work such a beautiful book and for their caring and friendship.

To William Packard who gave my long poems their opportunity and published more of my poems in *The New York Quarterly* than anyone else's. . . . To Richard Eberhart who invited me to read my poems at Dartmouth and wrote a foreword for "Crossing America". To Samuel J. Mandelbaum who typed my book *Another Poet in New York* and published it.

DEATH IN LOBSTER LAND

The publication of this book was originally aided by a grant from The State of Maine Commission On The Arts.

"Wawenock" and "From Five Islands Maine Rocks" first appeared in *Chicago Tribune Sunday Magazine*, Section 7, May 11, 1969 and November 22, 1970. "Sea Gulls Wait" appeared in *Granite* 11, 12, Winter 1977. "Origins" appeared in *The Goliards* 6, December, 1967, and in Redstart Plus, June, 1988. "Penobscot Raccoons" appeared in *Kayak* 44, Winter 1977. "Fair Warning" appeared in *The Maine Times*, and in Redstart Plus June 1988. "In Lobster Night" and "Lament for the Jews at Munich" appeared in *The New York Quarterly* 18, 1976, and 20, 1978. "Scott Huff" appeared in *Ploughshares* 4, No. 1, 1977. "Lament for the Jews at Munich" and "Scott Huff" were in the special New England issue of *Choomia Anthology* 11, 1977. "A Witness" appeared in Eric Oatman's *Manhattan Review*. "Garbage Truck" and "The End of the World" first appeared in *Paintbrush* 111, No. 6, 1967. "Hydrogen Now" appeared in *Dust*.

ANOTHER POET IN NEW YORK

"Lament for Federico Garcia Lorca", "The Moon Now Flushed", "Staten Island Ferry", "Helpless, We Go into This Ground, Helpless", "Violent Dying" all appeared in *The New York Quarterly*. "The Whole Thing about Jedge's House" appeared in *South & West*.

CROSSING AMERICA

"Crossing America V" and "Crossing America XXVIII" appeared in *Shenandoah*. "Crossing America XVIII" appeared in *Dakotah Territory*. "Crossing America XXIV" appeared in *Chicago Tribune Sunday Magazine*. "Crossing America XXV" appeared in *The New York Quarterly*. "Crossing America XXIX" appeared in the North American issue of *Exemplar*, Tübingen University, West Germany.

To the state of Connecticut Commission on the Arts for individual artist's grants that aided the writing of Crossing America and Massachusetts poems in 1974–1980.

MASSACHUSETTS POEMS

"Visiting Emily Dickinson's Grave" appeared in *Harper's* 261, No. 1566. "What Can I Leave for You to Feel of Me" appeared in *Choice*.

FOUR SHORT POEMS

"Through the World the Little Worm Forever" appeared in *Calvert* and in "The Leo Connellan Craft Interview", page 329 of *The Poet's Craft*, edited by William Packard, *Paragon House Publishers,*© by William Packard New York, 1987. "The Assassin" appeared in *The New York Quarterly*. "Boxing" appeared in *Red Fox Review* 4.

NEW AND UNCOLLECTED POEMS

"With Eberhart at Occom" appeared in *Choomia* 7/8. "York, Maine" appeared in *The Panhandler*, Spring 1985. "Ode to Karl Shapiro" appeared in *The New York Quarterly* 19. "Oscar Wilde Lament" appeared in *The New England Review/Breadloaf Quarterly* 11, No. 3. "Motel" appeared in *The New England Review/Breadloaf Quarterly* 6, No. 2. "To War Dead" appeared in *Dasein*. "The Treachery of Flame" appeared in *Another Chicago Magazine* 9.

THE GUNMAN AND OTHER POEMS

"As an Apple Has Iron" appeared in *The New Manhattan Review*.

PENOBSCOT POEMS

"Lobster Claw" and "Tell Her That I Fell" appeared in *Steppenwolf*. "Dark Horses Rushing" appeared in *The Georgia Review* XXII, No. 1, Spring 1968. "Watching Jim Shoulders" was published in *The Nation* 210, No. 5. "Shadows" was published in *The New York Quarterly* 6. "Closed Wake" was published in *Chelsea* 24/25. "Out Jim Moore's Window" appeared in *Chicago Tribune Sunday Magazine*.

ANTHOLOGIZED POEMS

"Wawenock" appeared in *Contemporary New England Poetry Anthology* edited by Paul Ruffin, Sam Houston State University Press, 1987. "Watching Jim Shoulders" appeared in *Traveling America With Today's Poets*, edited by David Kherdian, Macmillan, 1977. "Someday I'll Be Dead" appeared in *Do Not Go Gentle*, edited by William Packard, St. Martin's 1981. "This Is a Stickup" appeared in *From the Belly of the Shark*, edited by Walter Lowenfels, 1973. "To War Dead" appeared in *Where Is Vietnam*, edited by Walter Lowenfels, Anchor Books/Doubleday, 1967.

Preface

I never thought I'd live long enough to write many poems. There were wild, dangerous years drinking and hitchhiking, hoboing, bumming, years as a salesman. I owe whatever gentleness I may have to my mother who died when I was seven but gave me all she could, to my wife, Nancy, who gave me my chance, the opportunity of time, who freed me to begin and try to write poems and taught me to love cats and I owe my daughter, Amy, for being the child I always wanted and for becoming a lovely woman who fills me with pride and makes me think that perhaps I was some kind of real human being who has the right to deal with human anguish and with imagination.

The poet has to trust that readers will come to the poem, leaving room for imagination. All good writing is realized by us because of what the writer has written for the reader to fill in.

I have tried to create my own poetry. I think that now I understand that when Ezra Pound insisted "Make it new!" "Make it yours!" he wasn't being literal. But I was so asleep that for a long long time I thought that Pound meant exactly to be new and make the work your own original work. However, I'm advised that he meant you could be Henry Wadsworth-Longfellow and read Boccaccio's *Decameron* and filter the stories through your personality and come up with *Tales of a Wayside Inn* and that would accomplish Pound's rule. I was so dumb that I thought Washington Irving totally invented and created what he wrote, only to learn, like a child faced with the Black Sox scandal, that Irving's familiarity with German folk tales allowed his fertile imagination to take basic situations of German stories and recast them in the setting of Dutch New York.

I thought that since so many wrote in rhyme, perhaps if I could develop large, lyric narrative with the rhythm, the sound and music in the lines but not copy Robert Frost, my work might win its place and recognition. The truth is I don't have the talent to write the large, lyric poems Frost achieved in an iron maiden of rhyme. I don't have the brightness of genius that makes us all gasp either; I'm not Richard Eberhart writing "Withholding Irony" or "Of the futility of prayer aware" in his poem "1934" . . . or Tom McGrath writing "Rusting coulee moonlight" in his poem "Used up".

Here are my poems. They are either poems or they are not, it is for others to decide. The poet has to trust that readers will come to the poem. Poetry should never tell it all but should convey the poet's trust of complete strangers. If the poem is created successfully, everyone will come to the poem, no matter when it was actually written, and join the poem's success, help realize, fulfill the poem. Poetry should leave to the imagination of others the chance to conceive the poem and to totally "realize" it.

I am extremely disturbed by even the conception of an "official" literature. We must insist on imagination, risk, thinking you see something and going for it, letting the poem make itself whatever it wants, free reign to the imagination and heart or poetry loses a chance just sometimes to achieve greatness. Most of the time we fail. We write more failures than successes but just every once in a while we may succeed.

LEO CONNELLAN
Norwich, Connecticut

Death in Lobster Land

Wawenock

It is my night for tears.
Pine tree, umbrella of blueberries,
I am gone forever from Lime city,
vanished as though an Indian never
slid across Chicawaukee lake
like all night on a match flame.

Your old county road your
back alleys no longer
know me, the boy
who carried ball bearings
through them in the pockets
of his mud crusted knickers
to kiss marbles into the
slush of spring.

The houses that saw me
cut clothes lines in the
dark cowardice of halloween
pretend they did not, and
the Penobscot sea is
cold blue to my middle years.

Sea Gulls Wait

Sea Gulls at their
flush.

To the granite and lime country, lobster,
plush berries popping the hills, Maine,
my Maine of wild rhubarb, sweet spruce
and pine trees, dandelion greens pulled
fresh out of your front lawn.

Maine of agony, Maine of my blood
and flesh in your earth and ocean. Maine,
I love you, green forests, rugged water,
harbors whose beauty has washed
chaos from my thinking all these years
before I sleep.

Left because love was not understood
because I was not my father's son in the
pride of his heart and my mother gone dead
on me. Left rather than live
penal servitude outdoors, spirit crushed, joy
turned to broken nerves, left, because I am
of the world, not a vicious niche of it.

Sea Gulls on the edge of my mind's lid
since boyhood. I know you. Do not
wait for me. I will never be
your feast and yet you draw me. I am
set for the town but not you.

You draw me like a fascination with disaster,
an appointment I know I must avoid yet in the
subtlety of our chase I may slip after all
into your bills although all the north winds
cannot drive me into your mouths. I cannot see
how I could come to you. But I must
watch you every instant I breathe.

Winds blow drifts of snow scream my dreams
and you were calling Sea Gulls although I was inland
where the snakes of cities might strike asking

me for a match and when I put my hands into
my pockets cut my pancreas in half with a
blade. Death is only as far from us as it wishes.

I took their daughters. It is too much
for mothers, hawks coveting the bull.
There is no forgiveness from the fish wife,
the farm wife, dreaming their little girls
out of fields, off sea drudgery.

The mothers of daughters I took
would themselves like to kill me, Sea Gulls,
themselves, no one else would be allowed
to do it. It is too much that they could
not step in between me and their daughters.

They slept revenge but the opportunity caught them
asleep. How could a boy know of these set traps
and that is how I slipped through unharmed.

A girl I took as a toothpick youth
with all my blood rushed into my telephone pole
looks at me contemptuously because
a man would have taken her without promises
but I was a sneak in her dress.

Mothers and daughters you constantly haunt me and
I am never in your thoughts except when
you see me and would like to kill me.

Women, mothers, bearers of life, I cannot fathom you;
sufferers of the pain that arrives us all
and you do not know life.

But here I am again home in your grasp.
Why did I come back! Sea Gulls, gray and
white in your death your hovering striking
darting under sea water for the kills of
the life in oceans yet you were the
hope of land to ships coming in on their knees.

All the Sea Gulls come down
in their odor of seaweed
gray like faces of strokes snapping
fish bellied as infants gobble,

but without innocence and
the town still wolfing.

Let me go from this place! I am
wild violets crushed in their sweaty palms.
No one has changed. We are together again
in the never healed near fatal
atrocity of my youth.

I will rush from this place this town
where night and morning make no difference.
Invalids do well here and Sea Gulls.

I will leave the sadness of houses their paint split
by uncoerced winter. In each other's arms, love
as you and I know it, knifing our thighs
with twenty nails, no, here man takes
his husband's rights from women setting their lips
against the plunge.

Snow falls the smotherer of victims
who always escape, but not far, through
the high blue berries, yes, the corner beer
store, yes, to struggle fish in boats, yes, into
canning factories, breaking their lives in their youth, yes,
men scooped out as the lobster they go after where
Sea Gulls wait, to the grave, yes, snatched quick from
the pocket book of the undertaker and a whole life
shoveled into the earth forever in seconds.

Yet straight, with not crutch, no dulled
days, home flooded me, though it is no
home to me, but danger.

Drunk in Arizona desert there you were Sea Gulls,
perched on a speck of sand. You were the screeching
voice in the wheels of freights.

Crawling San Francisco in blind stagger
I thought you had flown down through the
bars of a couple of drunk tanks and
really had me.

Especially when it rained pouring Sea Gulls
come in from violent out to sea storms, there

were a flock of you Sea Gulls on the piers
of the Embarcadero and I thought to myself
they have me this time

Come Sea Gulls, come! I am weak now
in this instant of home like walking
the earth after my time. The town never
loved me but I have an ache for this place,
forever the pain is there.

So, try me Sea Gulls; shall we strangle each
other? Perhaps on the sea's rim, Vinalhaven,
island of gouged out quarries beyond
rich green Owl's Head trees salt faded
but unbending, suddenly nothing around us,
Sea Gulls, but open ocean and then the island
and beyond, the whole world through the fog:
shall we play with each other there? No?
In Rockland, you would rather dart for me there?
No? Then you are also coward enough to know your
quarry and I must not even have the end
I feel is mine in your throat.

Where does a man like me die? Probably
in a hallway when my heart finally explodes
not in Maine then home, no, not even
where the scent of the fern is your last breath
licking sea salt from your lips with your last tongue.

I came home to where the blood
of my ancestors colors the snow moon, oh
why did I come back!

Origins

Mother, Father told me you were
like an impossible lily
that does not need earth or drink
and lives forever in my mind
without ever wilting.

The whole New England town was with him
perpetuating your image
for my boyhood heart suffered enough losing you
to Forever at age Seven,
dumped from manhood's dawn
into my middle thirties believing
you were beyond my grasp.

Father never once broke the ribbon on
the packaged secret through to the end of his own life
he loved you that much.

Mother, I never saw you clearly
until during a visit home a friend
slipped her tongue through the long sealed
tight lips of the town code.

Unanswered pieces of my whole life
my senses instinct into place
from way back in the dark storage room of my recall.

As for the town, they wanted me to always
see you as an Angel floating where
religions tell me you wait for me.

Always now you will be exactly as Father described you
to me but now I can see you.

Love you far deeper for being no longer vague,
a perfect someone I could never deserve.

One has to feel flesh, now rotted in the earth
which bore and I know loved me.

Now to Father, I know you have already moved close,
coffins burst into each other's arms again,

as you did the night you made me, now
at last wrap your lover to you for always
and keep him whose love and loyalty to you
never faltered.

The only way I can thank Father, Mother,
is I have put away the bottle.

Penobscot Raccoons

Rushing raccoon sound
in Higganum wood.

And far off in Glen Cove,
Maine, raccoon rushing
sound through Jim Moore's
window in emphysema death
sound oceans make.

        Sea Gulls fast down
after sardines along the
wharves of the town. Herring
is vile odor on the blue.

In long sheds of Sardine factories
men push racks of thin rusted
scaley trays called flakes because
dead sardines lay on them and stick
in the hot ovens; human beings
rise early, long before cold black dark
is stabbed by orange morning and come
to earn their food pushing the loaded
flakes into big ovens in heat, men like
raccoons scurrying, rushing from the
heat, pushing the loaded flakes in to cook,
in and out, into heat and out all day
after women sitting across the conveyer
belt slice off herring heads and tails
and are paid for the speed they
can load up racks of the flake trays.
The fish do not know it, their
life strangled from them forced
into oxygen. What we live on kills
another as our head under the water
of their world kills us. . . . death no
surprise to Jim Moore. . . . death always
part of Jim as all newspapermen
fill rag paper with the ruthless cold

print of the man who drove
eighty miles an hour on
Rockland, Maine's Old County Road
and dumped himself and
three children into a
bottomless quarry.

Then raccoons were
frantic in air bubbles. . . .

In Higganum, Connecticut wood,
the sound raccoons make
rushing through houses
and flames of fire make
crackling on dry wood.

And screams as
the sea screams
through Jim Moore's window,
always the splashing sea, Jim
knew in that alert haunting instinct
which causes the intuitive to
sense death in serenity
that there is no earthly
happiness but only time
survival struggling
for just a touch of love.

But who lives
as if this is so, in
Higganum wood the
man's grandchildren. . . .

      Sudden rushing of
raccoons sounding through
my ears. . . . glass shattering
tinkling death sound far off
in quiet Higganum wood.

Fire, everyone trying to
save on oil, old fashioned
wood stove without
old fashioned experience.

Fire squeezing like
white paste from hot
old wood stove pipe lying
like a tongue on an icicle
rips flesh, flame
burst the baseboard.

In Higganum wood
the man's grandchildren
died but if it wasn't
an old wood stove with
its pipe too close
to dried wood of the house
you would have gone in
a hundred years anyway
or forty but I your
grandfather would not
have had to wake up from
my bed and there was the
Penobscot sea again like
raccoons rushing in my
ears and across orange lit
darkness in December cold
with the Christ child only
mangers away, children
trapped scurrying like
raccoons in an attic of flames.

Raccoons with
the ocean in my
filled head, Penobscot
raccoons in
Higganum wood, glass
tinkling and your screams
while fire tried
to burn down the sky.

And across the haze
of my eyes you died. . . . I
should have been gone, not you.
Your grandmother should have
been gone, not you, by

right we'd all be dead
before you, your mother's
breasts would not forever have
a stake of pain heavy between them
from aching for you, we'd
have been lucky enough to be gone
before you, but God has decided
that we must see you go
before we do, this is Hell.

Your father took
an ax to the old
wood stove because
something had to be gone after.

Fair Warning

Down the dark Pine green,
in deep blue quiet, the
flippers of sea waves
slapping inches off the shore.
Scent of deer moss and fern
soured, all the silence shattered
by the abrupt dog bark of gun blast
rapping the knuckles of water
that let a stranger's boat lie bobbing
and the foreigner lobstering!

Take my virgin daughter if
I don't kick your teeth out,
take my worn out woman
skinny on my provision,
but threaten our living, thief
in my salt flowing refrigerator,
I'll take your life.

In Lobster Night

I

Otto Fishinfolk, he's
everywhere you go.

Home, just off train,
to the house for a quick change
and that joy of first rushing
downtown to see Main street again.

Otto's there. "In N'York, aincha!"
"Yes, I am." "Like hit?" "I miss
home." "Ayuh, I know hit!"
"Well, see you Otto."

But no, "Hey now, you cummin'
with me tonight. We goin't'git laid."

You fear if you say no, the horror
of something you cannot conceive.

He can smell your fear of his violence
if you don't come and makes you go
with him stalking a night of lust.

In dark green
of the Lobster town.

Unable perhaps to face
really wishing to flutter.

He needs you violated, your
life happiness spoiled.

Devoured, you rush away from home
and forever the beauty is all dirty.

You come home drawn back by
need to come from some place
even after you got away.

The wild furious ocean never
said you could leave, the sea

like wrinkles in a turtle's neck
calls you back.

You come home and can't get away
from Otto, he's overwhelming, others
observing you two would resent you
with disgust that you don't stand up
for yourself, say no to Otto, that
you won't go with him.

But then he'd come after you
in a carfull of Ottos out of Port Clyde
to explode the boredom.

And you can't simply say
"Otto, I don't get home all
that often, have places, people
to see and spend time with my
father because our time together
is gone. The light in his winter
eyes is fading.

II

We were after the Kaylor sisters,
Otto parked and into Del's Pool Room,
cold cigar smell in spittoons, smoke
on pool table green.

Charlie Tyler playing points when
we come in, there was a thing 'bout
Leatrice Butler between Otto and Charlie, she
come to Saturday night good time with clear
understanding she leavin' with Otto once
"Four Haddocks And A Hake," his group finished
up with "Granddad's In Thomaston Wishin' He
Wusn't," but when Otto come to take her she'd
snuck out with Charlie. . . . what Otto wanted me
along now to see or do I didn't know, I was in
the horror of terror. Without seeming to move
Charlie slammed Otto on the forehead
with the back of his pool cue without
even turning or seeming to miss the rhythm

of his shot. Otto almost went down but he
didn't and the shoeshine air was full of death.

It screamed out of pool room silence
and was in everybody's champing hesitation
like lobster blood might get out of human skin.

My breath clotted
in the fury.

But it suddenly passed as though pre-arranged,
Otto said to Charlie Tyler 'I'll be wanderin'
-n-you know Leatrice Butler's mine to pass out
not yours to take, wimmin is special, still, when
I cum where you are, whallop me agoodun as I'd do by
you by Gawd when you're fed up with the sea and blueberryin'.

And so out of Del's on this horror, because Otto
had to have me know he could take anything he wanted
in Penobscot without leaving, who did I think I
was to leave. . . . you can be Postmaster's son or Kelsey
Fishinfolk's boy, but you're an outsider forever
because you left, evidently thought you were
better-n-everybody.

In dark bar called by every yearning boy "The
Passion Pit," blueberry pickers with fishingmen
off boats and Sardine people with the crumpled
green of their hard work going in two drinks of
a shot glass to twangs of Otto heading "Four
Haddocks And A Hake," possibly rendering "High Holin'
In Th'Blueberries". . . . he vents himself on victims
who yearn for his excitement in this dull place.

III

In the blood night of chaotic poverty
Otto took me to get the Kaylor sisters
in Union, to drive some place full
of pine and balsam smell in mosquito
heat and plunge into.

When we came into their home the lobster
moon turned orange, the parents looked

away as though they couldn't offer
much life to the girls and even if the
bible told them Otto was the devil, still,
if they wanted the sight of their children,
if they didn't want them to go die on the
lower East Side, or in the waters of
San Diego, they'd better say nothing.

The lust in me wanted their daughter
but my eyes could not look at them.
Strange, the sneak in my nature tried
to make believe now, to make it a
secret from the real me that I was
erotic and wanted her. The earth
in me wanted the girl, while I would
have protested in horror the rape.

The girls knew why we had come for
them and what they were heading to do
if they wanted Otto Fishinfolk and the
only excitement around Penobscot town
week-end nights when he stands center
at "The Pit" bludgeoning the world
with a guitar.

IV

We drove into green woods. The lobster
were shedding their claws. Little mosquitos
hovered over our sweat and had us like
over ripe fruit. In the woods, in dead
green, the dull dark green Maine winter
does to green, and murdered lobster
thrashing their lives out in the traps
of the bay does to green, taking the
bright life from the land that
allows death in the sea.

Otto stopped the car and said over his
shoulder to Rita Kaylor, "You takin' "
and she nodded, but it was his orders
she took, not me.

Already her sister Elvira Kaylor was
undressed naked and sobbing for Otto
who crawled on her chewing on a toothpick
while under me Rita was like a run away
plumber's snake, with her eyes closed, but
I didn't feel I was the lover she was
moaning to in lobster night.

But we were too big for the car, four
of us churning butter so I climbed
over her and was gone in the black.
She rushed out too, it was so good that
suddenly I loved Otto, a great surge
of the joy in hot lust, outside by the lake
I put her on the ground and she tickled
the sky with her toes while I extinguished
myself. Crushed rock sand cut my knee caps.
Cricket churp went quiet. Slipper sweat itched.
Suddenly a quiet fury in the used girls.
We were all stifled in sour let down.
It was awful by the lake now. There was no
wake for the death of ourselves.

Scott Huff

Think tonight of sixteen
year old Scott Huff of
Maine driving home fell asleep at
the wheel, his car sprang awake
from the weight of his foot head on
into a tree. God, if you need him
take him asking me to believe in
you because there are yellow buttercups,
salmon for my heart in the rivers,
fresh springs of ice cold water running away.
You can have all these back for Scott Huff.

By the Blue Sea

She used to walk by
the house of the boy she
loved hoping he'd see her
and come out.

Slowly she walked by, love
a spike in her wind pipe. . . . dry
throat ache and pain all
she got for loving the boy
who took her by the blue sea

but would not come out
of his house and take her
inside to keep

    He had no job or money, he
    wasn't supposed to be
    doing what they were doing.

He liked the love making
near rocks that jagged
up through flesh skinning sand,
but there was no way he could
come out of his house to her
when she walked slowly by.

Finally, she took a man who
had the same job the
father of the boy she
wanted had and so there!
But she didn't have him.

And her husband went
out every night, not with
women or to drink but
out on a boat, a Dragger, out in
dark ocean.

He was a mean husband and
furious. He bent the prongs
of a fork to show his

evil strength to her if
she crossed him, like by
bearing a daughter.

She bore him five sons
in six years, five sons
and only wanted him to
come home to her evenings
from his fine job as good
as the job the father of
the boy she loved and
couldn't have had.

But her husband didn't
see a woman telling him
how to live and went out
of Harbor, Maine on a
Dragger after Sardines,
Mackerel. . . .

> He's had what he wants of
> you Fish Woman so he goes
> out on a boat after
> other helpless things leaving
> you alone in pitch quiet, alone,
> his love is the fish lust of your carcass,
> and the stalking cowardice of illiterates
> who prey on fish who can't get away
> through slippery water. . . .

He liked being out on
the ocean with no people
coming in you got to wait on.

His clothes always smelled
of gasoline and fish.

And with his perpetual
dead cigar he always
smelled from combination
cigar fish and gasoline like
the smell from first touch
of a match to fresh cigarette

making young children
car sick. . . . he
was something to wait for
to crawl into bed with.

Well, all this time the
boy Fish Woman loved back
by the sea where Burdock
bushes stuck in his hair
like shot Porcupine quills,
boy she loved had failed
the pretentious pisspot aristocracy
expectations of his family
and those years from
time to time would stagger
in and out of countries and states
full of Molson of Canada or the
Ballantine of New York and
one evening in the dark
parking lot of a Damariscotta
dance hall he staggered up to her
and still even then to her
he was still even then one
of those lovely people she had
hoped to marry into and she
knew if he ever stepped
inside dance hall that night,
her husband, breaking ritual
and taking her dancing that night, hoping
to cure all this foolishness 'bout
his being home with her nights, her
husband would lay his eyes on
the boy she really loved and
at last have him victim
for all her imagined coldness
to him, now her husband would
beat the boy she loved into
hospital or dead and
that night under the
singing leaves of lust in a
dance hall parking lot Fish

Woman protecting mother of
staggering boy of the blue pines.

There in the cold moonlight
thinking thoughts like how
he could get her again, he actually
stood there and asked her if
she'd still go with him even now
if he finally came to her.

He babbled he'd take
her five children too. . . . her and
her five children. . . . She looked at
him sadly and smiled and said
she would, standing there knowing
he never would come for her but now
she knew it was because he was
a breathing dead man.

She never expected to
see him again where the
Pines came down there
ringing them in an
embrace of doom.

Well, she was a proud girl,
too alive to allow herself
to die in an empty house
where the man went
chugging out to sea nights.

Her beauty was English, the
Falcon nose, but
poverty showed in her set mouth.

And she had the guts
of women who stood
on Widow walks knowing
their men dead out through
the salt splashing fog.

And she left her sons
to save herself.

She tore herself from
her children to survive.

The way life was put to her
she has a right to, if she
could do it. . . . leave her children. . . .

            I hear the crying
            children at the
            loss of their mother. . . . little
            things sitting looking out
            windows at anything that moved,
            the wind, trees
            swishing and swaying
            expecting it was mama
            come home, but
            she never came.

The way her life was she
had to tell herself that
a woman wouldn't know
what boys need to know. . . .

It was a hard thing to do
leave her sons, I do not
judge lest someone see
me for what I really am, see!

Fish Husband who had the
same job as the father of
the boy she loved whose
house she used to walk
slowly by, Fish Husband
could go out off
on the sea and that
was alright. . . .

But for her to want anything
the least of which was to
simply have him home with
her in the dreary house at night
was supposed to be more
than her right.

And it was the usual
sorrow back and forth

You cannot make children
with someone and leave
just like that!

Back and forth, she
tried it again with the
man who had the same
job as the father of the
boy she loved, but once
something is broken it
is destroyed. . . .

                      and children are destroyed,
                      crying children, her
                      heart broken boys sitting
                      looking out windows
                      thinking since she
                      came back once she'd come
                      back again, but she didn't.

Once again she struck out
into the world of jibes, world
of hatred for people who
do not just accept their death.

Finally, again, she married
(you have to eat), a man who
was so happy to have her he
bowed to everyone in church
as they got married.

And Fish Husband she left, no
sooner was she gone, took
another woman to wipe
noses, clean and
cook for a flock, who
didn't mind his saddling
up and riding the
range of the sea, she had her
Charlie Pride records, who
soon presented him with

a little girl who completely took
over his heart, he was wild about
her, he, who had bent fork prongs and
shoving them under the nose of
Fish Woman Lurleen who used to
walk slowly in front of the
house of the boy she loved who
didn't come out to her. . . .

                Her boys grew up to
                tell her how as children
                they'd indicate their
                father's second woman
                as their mother, ashamed
                to tell anyone their real
                mother was alive divorced living
                up in Boston. . . . They didn't know
                how to tell anyone
                their real mother wasn't dead
                for leaving them.

Now, another life later, the
boy in some need, survived and
lived long enough to throw her
on her back again and climb on,
whatever, maybe just to find her to
erase those things that horrify our memory, now
one day the boy she loved all those years ago
by the blue sea. . . . now

one day the boy she
loved all those years ago
came to see what he could
get or regret but her
second husband was fresh cold
and going with him wouldn't
look right, besides love is
hatred when used or ignored.

. . . . "I loved you once"
she told him now without feeling,

she told him from way deep inside like
there was a little her inside herself
calling from long ago. . . . "I loved you once."

Calling "I loved you once" now
to him like retreating
surf of ocean spraying as
waves come in from way back deep.
Her face did not move
and it was a voice
of love that had died walking
past his house hoping he'd
come out, that said to
him now. . . . "no more, no more, but. . . . I loved you once."

Now when he looked up at her,
she putting horror in
him, sinking feeling, she told
him he picked a day to
find her, her
second husband who bent
over at the middle so
glad was he to get her,
dropped dead and that
his coming now made her
feel that the sudden
massive coronary death
of her second husband must
be punishment for her

         leaving her children, for
the times he and she they
lay under pines by
the blue sea. . . .

                      She told him she
                      used to lie pregnant
                      fearing the babies
                      would come out with
                      three heads because
                      of what he and she

         did by the pines
         near blue ocean all those
         years ago, even in snow, by
the blue sea frosting
each other's eyes with our breaths.

Edwin Coombs

Edwin Coombs is dead.
I just saw him.

And I talked to him on the telephone.
But he's dead.

I see Edwin fresh home from
the Marines, the Second
World War over and I'll be
getting out of Rockland, Maine
High School soon. We've got a
lot to talk about, plans to
make. . . . he's dead!

In anguish I think everything,
imagine him murdered!

What occurred!? Undoubtedly nothing
but freak tragedy fluke of circumstance
and it is my broken heart reacting.

What happened!
What does "Falling in love" mean?
Marrying Betty Grable face, Jane Fonda
backside, Jane Russell breasts, but
not a person.

Our life for fantasy people
willing to put out for another
victim, shall we
make my boyhood friend's
death, murder?

I could say in my grief that
his wives murdered him, the
first one, say, not living
long enough to accomplish his
death, he, unaware she
wanted him dead but after
a long time at her pleasure,

he, unknowingly proceeding
to choose the woman who would
be his widow to marry, but why
would she kill him, why should she,
how! . . . . By needling him? . . . . until
finally exasperated he
sprang to death, not suicide
but self death of anyone marrying
face and body but not the
person who "realized"
it, that they were
loved for what they looked like,
not themselves, perhaps
unconsciously, but more
likely cold bloodedly exactly
retaliating for that awful
kind of feeling being used as
a lust receptacle rejected
visualizing ourselves as
loved frantically, sweaty
loved, jerked in, like a
bicycle Tire Pump is loved,
petted, fondled by the sweaty
anticipating hands while
it fills up the wheels making
possible ego satisfying rides
even as he ejaculates in you
with his eyes closed so you
never know who he's dreaming
of as the hot splattering of
loads rests him on you a
hulk ready to snore which
would be alright if you knew
he loved you but what he loves,
if indeed he loves at all, is
your Betty Grable face, Jane
Fonda backside, Jane Russell
breasts. . . . he never conceives
you're onto his fantasies and
out for vengeance in your

disgust so is bewildered
as to why being with you
is no longer fun but deadly.

He does not comprehend
it is deadly until he
is dead, then, up floating
over himself he knows, but
like a balloon the air
is let out of he's
swishing off into the gone.

None of us ever saw
much of Edwin after
he married.

He trusted that woman
for something he thought she'd
"see" he needed and give
him, he wasn't self sufficient
and she broke him and he
liked it. It hurt and was
warm, violent and sensual
and that first wife helped
him fail which he couldn't
stop himself from needing.

I had not seen Edwin
for a couple of years ever
since the small difference
of age between us was
caught up and I had been
away in a uniform too, back,
I stopped by his married home.
It was forboding, dark,
bleak and he met me shuffling,
taking the tack that I was
still young, single, wouldn't
know the new rule of living
on a man when he gets married.
But we had been very close
so he couldn't bring himself
not to take me into the house

and introduce me to the woman.
She was a quiet one, absolutely
physically beautiful
in an olive way and cold.
However I could see making
love to that face, that
mouth, that body and she
saw I could, suddenly
smiling that such lust
was possible for my life.

I know Edwin saw clearly
the bargain we might be
striking but he slunk
out of the way turned
not to interfere. This
was all part of the
warm hurt violent and
sensual she inflicted
on him as part of their
relationship which he
liked like children with
freshly spanked bottoms
often seem to need to
throw their arms around
their beaters as though
for agreement, reassurance,
they've been hit and now it's
over and they can at least
count on the relationship. . . .
What did she have that held
him, something! He stayed
with her twenty years until
she died. . . . She had
planned him dead but
his luck was her death.
Perhaps it was his
Yankee New England
morality or guilt that
held him with her but
more like need, she was

punishment, something he
needed.

She was a quiet one, dark of
mood, cold, vicious. Edwin's
friends never saw him about
after she got him, once he
married that woman, no,
never in Del's Pool Room
anymore or in "The Passion
Pit" with the boys drinking
with a girl from Saint George
or from Hope, a big cigar
in his teeth, his head in
a stetson biting the
big cigar, grinning,
talking hard, ready to fight
enjoying the feel of the open
hand slapping someone
and the head clearing slap back.
I used to be hanging along
in the shadow of legendary Edwin
waiting for his hard guy type
of remark through clenched
teeth and follow him with a
crowd of the boys up into
hotel room for fun with
Fish Women from over to
South Warren; once they were
all spread out on the floor
Southern Comfort full and
I was the only one who could
move, so later Elvira Camiston
from down th' harbor told Edwin
 . . . . "That young-un with th' ears
he's goo-ud! Bring him next
time, Edwin, he c'n pump
like hell-n-cum off too!"

 . . . . Realize Edwin's widow
as the kind of woman he
needed. . . . no matter what

egged him Edwin got up out
of that Sunday afternoon
chair all by himself
and dashed out to death.
No other's arms forcibly
lifted him nor was he
dragged by force. . . . what
gave way in him, what
blocked his comprehension
like a Pittsburgh steel
worker climbing right into
blast furnace roaring flames he
reaches cold steel in to melt
the only time iron weeps.

. . . . Some survive by devouring,
but then he chose women for
what he wanted from them and
would rather have it than his life.

He wouldn't admit that but he
cautioned me no four letter
words or any remarks that
would mean she wouldn't
let me come again. Edwin,
a grown man of 53 said that
to me.

In his home, when we met
after years, after a long time
Edwin showed me two hundred
year old rooms and told me
plans that sound like he
didn't need her, the way
youth, boys will talk about
camping and fishing, outdoor
hunting trips without thought
of a girl in them and when
woman is in their lives,
often never talk that way again.

Edwin Coombs said to me the things
he had not done but would do, that

afternoon I saw him once more
once again after a long time.

When I saw him after years
his face was like sifted ashes.
I remember the blond handsome
youth with sensuous lips and
amused self confident strutting.

I remember thinking
as I saw him after a long time
. . . . he looks dead, the blood looks
sucked out of his face like his
life raw egg through punctured shell
is going only by a beat.

What is happening here for
my eyes to see if they will!

Probably nothing it is
only my heartbreak. . . . still
he looked grey like a man might
look if he thought to himself
in his head he was dead. . . . if
the situation of his living
was become so bad, he was
grey like that.

But we know his widow,
no one could meet a finer woman.
She is the survivor of three men.

Why should she kill him! She didn't!
I am heart broken and looking for anything
to blame, anyone, my boyhood
friend is gone.

And it is my broken heart falling on
a good woman, no better, no worse
than any of us, lovely, beautiful
to see and assume.

My boyhood friend is dead
and I am full of grief

which for a cold one like me
is forgotten experience.

I remember when I visited
she looked at me sourly,
contemplatively, her lips
clamped down making her
nose look bulbous and
slightly to the left
as if annoyed by the
possibility of the one someone
or something that could
jerk Edwin out of her control.

Coming into the house I sensed
her wondering if she must
match wits with me so I
played simpleton to look
to her incapable of comprehending
and since, luckily, some of us
are so foolish as to think
others do not see us exactly
and clearly and that our life
is the toleration of others,
her eyes took a look at me
and dismissed me and in order
to be with Edwin again, I
threw up the invisible mesh
veil of monopoly conversation
and sure enough she said to
me later . . . "You know, you
took over so, Edwin felt
completely left out. He wanted
to talk too, to show you some things."

But I felt that was better
then for her to feel threatened
by me so I wouldn't be
welcome to come see
Edwin at all anymore.

She, absolutely physically
beautiful, married twice

before she met Edwin, twice
survived little boy chauvinists,
the man she had her children
by had such an accident off a
diving board as to completely
paralyze him for life. He
was alive, could blink his
eyes, talk; somehow her
son, a little child at the
time, was given the burden
of the blame for the man's
diving board accident. . . .

. . . . as if there wasn't enough
water in the pool to dive into
and it was a small boy's fault!

. . . . as if thick ropey weave
diving board was soapy slippery
and it was a small boy's fault!

. . . . Who knows how a strong young man
became broken to pieces! But
for the sanity of everyone
she didn't stay around to
carry any bedpans, no, she
married a man she wouldn't
have if she'd see how
infuriated a woman like
her made him, a woman who
abruptly shut him off and took
to her bed loaded on pills
so later no one could ever
demand to know why she didn't
come out and face an issue, he
went into rages when
he "realized" her and
in put him in a mental hospital.

. . . . Someone will think
"She's not a very good woman,
didn't stay with the diving board man,"

have human compassion. . . . who ever
had any compassion for her!?

Where did her hatred begin!?
. . . . if, in fact she wasn't born
cruel in her nature, if man
created poison in her, when!?
As a little doll on a man's knee
with his fingers feeling up
under her dress. . . . Did a
gang of men get her out
in horrible whistling green
of dance hall woods with
Glenn Miller's "Moonlight Serenade"
drowning out her calls for help while
they pumped murder into her.

But where does evil come from?
What could make a beautiful woman
hate so much that she'd allow her
own male son to have his life scarred
feeling he was responsible
for an accident that broke
his father like grass. . . .

. . . . if she couldn't get the boys
who got her she'd make one to get
and she'd get everyone, every man
she ever could. . . . the first thing
she told me she did, that time
I saw Edwin again after a
long time, right after she
married Edwin they went
to a gathering of Antique
Dealers and publicly she
just picked up some antiques
and put them onto the back
of their truck, stole
antiques and put them in
their truck knowing they'd
be kicked out of the Antique
Dealers' Association, but

that was getting Edwin right
from the start, just so he got
in case, apparently, her luck
ran out, something prevented
her usual plan.

I was appalled hearing it, but
more by the way Edwin just
stood there hearing her tell
it to me and laugh like
it was really a smart stunt, he
just stood there and took it, she
was his pin-up girl with
Betty Grable face in a
bathing suit hiding Jane Fonda
backside and those
Jane Russell breasts almost burst
through swimming suit,
lugged around in U.S.
Marine duffle bag and
pinned up on walls. . . . when
Edwin saw her it was 1943
again, and the sadness is
he meant her no disrespect,
would like to have loved
her inside as a person but
he didn't understand and
could have died believing
that she "knew" what she
looked like and "was
completely satisfied" that
he loved her face and
figure which had always
been yearned for ever
since she could remember,
lusted after to strains of
Glenn Miller's "Moonlight
Serenade" but after
years of it, even in this
liberated "Ms." feminist
time, she really got to

the point where she almost
wouldn't have minded some
unshaven man saying to
her "Come here, Broad!"
or "if you want to know
where the Public Library in
Bangor, Maine is, Babe, you
get up off your butt,
drive to Bangor and ask
a cop!" It really would
have been a change. . . . a
"crude" change, and no one
likes being referred to
as a "Broad," but, still
someone might be talking
to her as flesh and blood
woman instead of as the
last male symbol,
visualized as men wanted
her and she had the
strength and courage to
leave relationships and
push herself above the
male idea, to survive it,
even if that involved a
little smashed death here
and there, a great woman!

Edwin so frail
even as a young man
back from the Marines, he
affected cockiness but
wavered even staggering
in his voice, you
almost expected him to
crumble to dust and vanish.

All us High School boys heard
stories about his legendary
cock prowess, a "must" in those
days to be important in the
Lime town, but I tell you

he was more like the
snapped stem of a tulip
than any steel rod.

He could be moved to
sudden violence and then
kill you with his fists
if you riled his sensibilities.
But if he loved you, you had him.
He would put up with
anything for love, abuse if you
cuddled him after the punishment.

If you were his comrade too
you had him, he could never
conceive you'd harm him.

Who knows what occurred!
It was so impulsive
like people drinking getting
slowly splashed and someone
comes in excitedly yelling
 . . . . "There's a man over in
your woods helping himself
to a Christmas tree cutting down
one of your Evergreens". . . . and
the way Edwin dashed
out in his car to middle
of main highway and
seemingly oblivious
of the danger, makes
one wonder who needled who
to rush after some
man cutting down a tree. . . . was
it worth your life
to stop someone ending
a tree's life?

You know how sundown
sets you up, blood green
of evening dark when
day drops behind a
fan of dusk. . . . Edwin

Coombs, my boyhood friend
heard in Christmas time,
man on his land to
cut trees with no
permission and you can't
just have what your eye takes
so he went outside with his
wife to protect what was theirs
and in that wanton way we
go cruising his car slid
along main highway breakdown
lane until he saw the man, and he
leaped out of his car burst
vehemently into middle highway at
night's coming when the
evening sits down on your life.

I can see him as he looked
before death ran him over his
head cocked like he was
cuddling his shoulder with
his cheek of a healed broken neck,
he always looked a broken bird
put together again. . . . now
gesturing oblivious of where
he stood as a driver who would
never remember death borrowing him
to steal Edwin in that low twilight
just as dark takes your eyesight;
my boyhood friend become ashes
scattered now somewhere over home.

A Witness

Sea Gulls beating wings
I saw you dying.
The sun turned its back
and I was driving
when you fluttered on the sidewalk.

Come in close from twenty straight days of rain
over the cruel ocean
to seek food where storms dump our refuse
open for the picking;
flew into a wall you did not understand
that springs on all of us
who might have won
alone and unsurrounded, fighting,
if we knew what was to be beaten.

Amelia, Mrs. Brooks of My Old Childhood

        I

Amelia, Mrs. Brooks of my old childhood
I have come to you again.

I was job training in
New Jersey and a letter
came from someone
we did not know.

I asked my wife to
read it to me over
the telephone in
vague, irritated curiosity
and it was from someone
I had never heard of, your
Sister-in-law.

She admonished you loved me so much I
ought to be ashamed at my neglect of you, all these years.

        II

      "No-o, Amelyuh duzzent
live withus. . . . No-o, Amelyuh's
across th'bridge t'Brewer, in a
nice nursing home. . . . a nice! nursing home-n-her boys
live near by. . . . No-o, Amelyuh don't know
y'cummin'. . . . I wrote you. It was
my idea. . . . I'll go telephone her now!
Y'gut a minute haven't you!? You'll go
see her!?"
    . . . . This one resents! She
can't put her finger on it but there's
something in the loose free easy
way I materialize at her door from
miles away within a week of receiving
a letter she just dashed off for
whatever reason. . . . or was it
overwhelming for her to write. . . ?

        She can't put it
into words but what it is is her kind
has lost control of me. I move in and out
and around them as I please and if I
please. . . . I got away. . . . she knows
I got away!

        From thin foundationless houses
plunked onto the earth, to the left a little from
Maine winters, like the old bow legged ladies inside,
sagging on teacher's pensions and dying in a rut
unable to even take a car trip because gas and motels
cost, stuck in the house for life, the only thing in
their lives now, dragging out to supermarket for
hamburger to make endless never changing meals of
meat cakes, peas, mashed potatoes cold in their pepper and salt
with the never melted butter clinging like a car that
has skidded on ice under snow to the side of a snow bank.

III

Great lady of Sardines and
earth and blood of
Blueberryin' years, Clam Factory
years who brought up
children without help, a hopeless
drunk husband beating you in
his futility when the country was smashed.
Amelia, lady of poverty and no hope,
saint of this earth if ever there
is a saint and if not then you
are what was always instilled in us
as what a saint is, woman in the
retinas of God's eyes for your simple courage
and great accomplishment with no money
and from work that kills young, yet
you still live, Amelia, and here we are.

I came to you the day I
went into the army
        where sardines stuck

to your hands I came and said
goodbye in the fish smell.

You were beautiful, a
beautiful woman and
I yearned to say goodbye
to a mother.

You worked the Sardine Factories
        to feed your children.

No fish contributes
more to the human
race as Herring.

        We sneak death again,
        kill. . . . take
        herring from the sea our
        boat circling, the Cannery
        boats lifting the sardines
        aboard into their holds
        through hoses.

A Seine around
fish in moon black.

Draw string of net
pulled to close the
net bottom or the
fish sucked through hose. . . .

        To the Cannery as
        soon as fish are
        aboard, Herring
        through a hose removing
        their scales for imitation Pearl
        essense on the Market Place
        and Cosmetics.

        IV

Amelia, the fish have less
chance than you had
except your death would

be more subtle, you died
from it, Amelia, died from exhausting
survival, your life wearing
out your life.

                . . . . no machine can pack sardines
                like human hands, Amelia. . . .

          to feed your children.

Sitting in draughty cold
snipping off dead fish heads and tails
        with scissors.

      Yet death always a sneak, here
is food to eat but it will decompose
if we do not know that herring who have
just eaten must be allowed to swim it off until
they digest whatever was in them as you catch them. . . .
or whatever they were eating avenges them as
bacteria planktonic form. . . .

And once caught out of the fresh salt
protecting ocean if the fish are taken
distance of more than four hours they spoil,
Amelia. . . . life is death all spoiled.

              V

Amelia, did you go north
in the few years of the Winter Fisheries
to Eastport-Lubec, Maine, freezing
nets of two and one half inch mesh
sunk to the bottom in twenty
fathoms of water, fish catch
frozen solid on the market as "bloaters."

Amelia, sitting in frigid
cold icy sea water splashing
and wind finding you through
building cracks.

The cooked fish come down
conveyor belts for you to

pick up without breaking them
and put them into cans of
oil or mustard, fast!
You were fast all day
or out of work. . . .

                    to feed your children.

And to feed your children, bending in
Blueberry fields making your numb
fingers pick fast
to fill up pails quick
without bruising the blueberries
or you'd be out of work!

Vaccinium, that shrub
growing wild on barren uplands
of Maine bearing clustered, mild
sweet tasting fruit either blue
or purple black and coated with
greyish powder. . . . Amelia you were
paid not by the time you
spent raking your bony hands blistered
slippery flesh but by the amount
you raked. . . . There is no other way
to harvest blueberries other than to
bend over from the waist, tough back,
strong wrists, the strength
put in you by your children to
feed, to pull for, pull
pick through blueberry bushes
with a gentle rocking motion. . . .

                    to feed your children.

Amelia, how could you love
Maine, the blood blue ocean,
the black green pines and
fresh yellow and green
dandelions with your nose
plowed in the earth or
in the stink of the
dead of the sea.

> Although you were no whore
> you were as exploited
> and paid for piece work. . . .
>
> to feed your children.

VI

And into Clam Factories

> to feed your children. . . .
>
> At night you'd take
> hold of one of your hands with the other hand
> and grip to squeeze out the pain of
> Clam shell tiny cuts so you could sleep. . . . to
> be able to get up another morning to
>
> feed your children.

And all you ever said anything
about was your sorrow at no time
or opportunity for education to be
accredited a nurse for the bed pans you carried
to feed your children. . . . and assist the almost dying
whose saved lives never knew you were ignorant.

VII

In my lost mother boyhood
I stumbled over her kitchen cookies.

Now I am written
where she is in this world.

Her face is now under a spider web.
I have to look hard for
my memory to find it but
her voice is still
that inflection I remember.

> She looks at me with
> mixed emotions at best. . . . if

I ever loved her at all then why
have thirty years gone without a
word from me, no note, never
a Christmas card. . . .

        Because she
is not the obligation my mother
would be. . . .

                I would not have you know, Amelia,
                my years struggling to be my own me
                and not what would please others who
                would be under a head stone just
                when I needed them, just as
                our love affair was coming

And I called out

        "Here I am the way you wanted me". . . . but
they were not there.

VIII

Amelia, Mrs. Brooks of my old childhood, I
have come to you again.

I was suddenly told where
to find you and I broke
New England until here
you and I are again, here
we are both of us in your
little apartment.

We both have died since
we've seen each other.

You speak to me now
and we both feel uncomfortable,
ours is a relationship of wish.

You tell me deaths and
I tell you deaths. . . .
They almost killed us both
when they happened but telling

is embarrassing like what
are we talking about!

We have always lived
under the belief
that there is no help!

IX

.... One of your sons, I remember him, Bob, I
served Mass with him on altars of
sour wine on early morning air and
bad breath smell from orifice emissions
in the middle of fervent prayers
and closed windows. . . . Bob
tripped into an airplane propeller
instead of flying the plane
home for Thanksgiving.

Yet you tell this to me without
even a wince or remorse of
the anguish in your
voice or expression. . . .

Because just going through
bringing him up
wore out your tears. . . . long ago.

You lived through days you
never thought you'd see
the end of and yet
tomorrow was no relief.

And I do not react
either, death
will finally be my death.

It is strange to think you loved me,
the way you told your
Sister-in-law

        "I just love that boy!"

You would like to love me I
was a boy with no mother and

you had no one either
and often thought of dying and
leaving your children
without a mother. . . .

It makes you believe
you love me and
in your old years the
memory of little me running round
may make you believe
you love me.

X

Now in this midnight of
my lost mother boyhood we may
never see each other again.

        A letter appeared telling me
where you were and since I
found myself still alive I
came to you once more. . . .

        The sea is in
your voice and my life is
etched in the lines of your face.

If a woman like you wants to
think she loves me, take me
again in your heart in my old childhood.
For soon earth will cover us.

Garbage Truck

Man built scavenger come
at firing squad time, the
low time of morning
when we most need to be loved
lest we rave our streets screaming
from the piled up truth.
We turn our sleek bellies to balloons
full of canned dead things and lie
wheezing in each other's arms
calling the grave until
it answers.

In Maine We Own Our Sea

On a tombstone in Thomaston, Maine cemetery
are letters spelling out my ancestor
carved like doughnuts in granite. All the sea
did not get was his name. It was before the
Rockland Breakwater holding ocean undertow
with a stone Judo punch.

In the old days as the boats came in at sunset,
fatigue on the faces of worn out winners
told us the sea had lost. Now the ocean will never win.

We own our sea in Maine. We rode the highest bucking wave
and broke it with the big engines of our power boats
throwing oil in the eyes of the tide.

Now fish fly ice packed to Berkeley, California,
green profit floats down through our pines, and our
graveyard is slow filling in this infancy of earth orbit.

Blueberry Boy

I only wish I could have it just once more,
you go back and the place looks dull and
small in its mosquito biting green.

I was a Blueberry boy in that childhood,
the sun would flush my freckles out
from where winter hid them in the
sallow pale color of snow and I would
run the meadow for blueberries that
my aunt Madge would turn into muffins
I have longed for down the tripup of manhood.

Just a minute again, on my knees, picking
frantically with expectant watered tongue,
ignorant of what lay out of the woods.

From Five Islands Maine Rocks

The wrinkled sea lined with
near dying experience like faces
of toads, survived as ice
water too cold to perish slips
out to tip over ships and wrestle
the sailors down to its tomb and
I know this land rugged with
the insides to outlast whatever nuclear
springs tomorrow out of its powder-puff.

What I breathe is clear and sharp to
snap my wits again as man
when there was no help but his two gnarled
hands shaping dreams to his own making.

From Five Islands Maine rocks where
Perry-Winkles crouch in pools of low tide ocean,
I am myself renewed to kick terror aside and
make a world again where people do not run
but shape a forever instead of our universal end.

Hydrogen Now

Is that was
isn't is it?
Is that isn't now
is frightening
isn't it?

Lament for the Jews at Munich

How much do you
want a country!

I ask you, how
much is your earth, land,
a nation that is yours worth.

How much! Here were
the cream of broken udders.

The dying cows calved
and here they were.

Here were the cream of cripples
tortured and destroyed who
refused to perish and vanish
and had the astonishing ego
to come back to Germany again.

And everyone knew that
Arabs were there too.

So, how much do you want a
country!

How much did jews
dehydrating to death
in Cuba's harbor want a country!

And jews stripped of
everything telling jolly fairy stories
to their babies clutched in their arms
while christian gas came out of showers.

How much did they wish
that their dying would be
for a country!

Salamon paid for George Washington's
army, the jews wanted a country so much.

You say you love the United States,
and I think you think you do, the

conception of giving up your own child
to slaughter in front of your eyes
as a price for your country has
never really been presented to you.

You claim you love the United States,
and I believe you love what you understand.
You wear hard hats with the American flag,
like it doesn't exist unless you paint it
and wear it in prejudice as you sing
the Anthem before ball games full of nigger stars.

Still, how much do you
really want a country!

It's hard protecting a virgin
forever one's own, along her borders
and in her heart.

You really have to want a country
or it's hardly worth what you
have to put out to keep a
woman who is your mother land
from being ravaged and obliterated.

Now, the IRA Irish guerilla
is a man who says goodbye to
his mother in the morning
and the next time he sees her
is when he blows her apart
in the supermarket he's mined.

But it hasn't won him his country,
it has only murdered his mother.

You have never wanted an Israel
so badly that to keep the dream realized
you would yourself direct the slaughter
of your blood comrades, sobbing,
retching for their lives behind blindfolds
as you directed their deaths.

Because if you once start
conceding, it keeps up
until you have no country any more.

Everyone knew
the Arabs were there.

We want this, you
want this.

You are only thinking how you
can participate without being known.

Like bouncing Ping Pong balls,
talking casually while just a
bunch of jews are being led
right by you to die.

Nothing keeps happening
that mankind does not want.

As long as it is not you
who is dying or having the bottoms
of your feet beaten until it shifts
your skeleton while you are
still alive breathing in it.

What will we do when our wars
are gone now that we do not
even have legal execution in the
death houses of our prisons. . . . what
will we do with ourselves. . . .

Everyone knew the Arabs
were there. . . .

Everyone knows that nothing
will be done.

The End of the World

They have seen the lobster water go dry.
Cold is the empty salt ocean in wake.
The lobster have been scooped out and are gone.
No more do empty baited traps fill.

Greed has drained the sea of its orange fruit.
Now the hard working men who wore themselves out
rising early and ripping the palms of their hands with rope
have time to go bathing like tourists.

Their taut wiry muscles will sag like unwound violins.
And they are dying looking at the ocean with nothing in it
  to go after.
The lobsters may be gone in Penobscot forever, certainly
putting out the traps again now will not bring them back.

Another Poet in New York

Lament for Federico Garcia Lorca

In the early dawn bleak cold
without sunlight,
They smashed the Butterfly
against a wall.

Yes, I know we are only children,
children picking up the smatterings
of what we can.

That brutal morning
the capes of Spain
folded themselves in shame.

We are children
who were not there,
know nothing of it.

But there are those among us
who even while we are children
put the eyes out of kittens,
tie Cats' tails together and
toss them over a clothesline
feeling warm pleasure
witnessing their frantic clawing
each other to death.

We will be the ones
who will do it again.

In all likelihood
the boys among us
will grow up and marry the girls
trying endlessly to prove our manhood.

Some of us never can.
We will always think it is in question,
that all eyes focus on us as un-men.

We will murder anyone
who does not feel a need to prove it,

is such a voice that birds
stop in flight in air to listen.

He is in the veins
in which Spain's Conquistadores' blood
reached its bouquet.

His precious singing words
of such magnitude
they clutch our breath.

Yes, I know we are only children,
children picking up the smatterings
of what we can.

He was whisked out of his house
as dawn was breaking,
his eyes deprived of one more sun
before forever dark.

Killed because he
wore skirts in the heart of his trousers.

We will let it happen again,
when the time comes
some of us will do it.

We are children
who could see to it, it did not
but we will not.

Would not want to be of them
who smashed the Butterfly against a wall
and the Courvoisier of his mind
wasted forever at only age thirty-six.

Whatever is the good to talk to children
who will do it again.

Federico, Garcia, Lorca . . . some of us
some of us are heartbroken. . . .
They do not make enough candles
in all the world's churches
to burn for you.

Not enough Rosaries can be said
or Acts of Contrition.

Because I know
it will happen again.

Conscious

Amphisbaena go me East
and slip among the unconcern.
There and come back here win
because I know how to kill.
And yet melt excited upon even
just seeing Margot Fonteyn
or a Dandelion for that matter,
white puffed coming apart in the
brutal air.

Mommy's Hubby

We were drinking buddies in high old time town
womb warm with Billie songs and Bird jazz,
so I put you up when you asked me now, but
you blew it when I filled the refer Ale full against my wife's
  frown.

      She has seen me like we were
      and my marriage cartwheeled for a minute.

          Hey, buddy, the wind avoids
          flashing his cape of zest at me.

How come you think the chicks still die downstairs for Jackie
  Levine!?
Jackie Levine has shot his last load in a young head.

          Jackie, Jackie Levine, Captain U.S. Cavalry
          Falling all over the Pacific, leaving his wife
          to finger herself, with a glue hairdo
          up in perpetual pin curlers,
          America's love-starved sweetheart dried up like
            a prune
          being true to Jackie Levine, dashing warrior.

And the mandolins were playing for hard-nose Fisk.
his red nose shines a medal from all the whiskey companies,
but the bottles are all broken in city dumps
full of Seagulls and stink.

          Our youth went out in tapped beer-keg blasts,
          spread-legged chicks where are you, wives of
          upstate doctors taking it on your sun decks
          behind shrubbery concealing freeways?

          You liked it in an East Side dump
          giving your cries to old men
          through cockroach paper-thin walls.

And I am Willis Fisk again
creeping streets to my job and crawling home.

> It gets over sometime, when?
> why do we wait!
>
> We wait waiting to find out what we waited
>   for,
> then we're quite willing to leave.

    Hey, buddy, you remember that sweet young thing come into Johnny Romero's on Minetta with oranges for a nice tight little ass so pot high she didn't know who you was next morning after we both banged her so drunk we never knew if we got off or not and she looked at us through her shades like we were creeps.

    Hey, buddy, remember Jerry's on the Bowery where I'd get a three-day kick washin' dishes and after fly for Thunderbird and Fanny'd come by with a bottle of green gin and maybe money to blot out horrible Sunday and you'd turn on your charm talkin' until finally dawn. . . .

> I remember, sure I do.
> I lie awake seeing it
> in the snore dark of marriage.

Now, you come to my house as though Billie was still singin'
  "Easy Living,"
The Bird still blowin' in high old time town.

> In the face of my old lady who saw me through
>   all the galloping hee-hee's,
> well, Jackie Levine, I have to say so long.

>> Yes, it's Fisk tellin' you split.
>> Imagine it, Fisk tellin' you leave!

Because now I'm Mommy's Hubby and we've got our coffins
  picked out
    plots and perpetual flowers.

The Moon Now Flushed

Across America the
young men were
throwing their
serial numbers away,
and some were sticking
their thumbs out along
the highways hitting
the cities broke.

And always Fry Cook
and Counterman jobs in
the cafeteria chains or
loading freight cars
with empty beer cans at
the American Can company.

You learned to buy and
carry with you your own
skillet that scrambled eggs
would never stick in, which
could put you out of work,
and a small pot for poached
eggs, your own equipment,
black tie and cummerbund so
you could get into a town
like Seattle with your girl
with you, put her some place,
in just a room to start, walk
into a spoon and go right to
work if there was any
job as a waiter,
dishwasher, counterman,
fry cook. Meant an
immediate meal for you,
meant money now.

The whole world hadn't
exploded. Boiling, but
the roads were still open

and the young girls
like the exciting kernels
of corn to strip their
green stalks down.

Blood of my dreams, I just
thought I saw you again when
the moon now flushed
across the pane of my window glass.

Now the daffodils were pushing
their daisies. It was the
last hour that blacks cringed.
My boyhood went when you did.

The last time blacks shook, yes,
before, I'm hip, they got wise
to why the old revolutionaries
tagged themselves Yankee,
Yankee Doodle and the sharpest
blacks realized all at once,
like all sudden realization,
that their pride lies in Nigger,
the tag to shout, to give themselves
back, Nigger like Yankee Doodle went
to town and Nigger he went too,
is going to town.

The cities were not yet exploding
in violence. Young men seeking
their women, blood of my life.
The grief of thinking of you now
almost shuts off my breath.

Going through girls to
find you. Neither of us knew
that love is taking punishment
while giving the other hell.

Young good-looking black men with
megaphone voices drank themselves
to death because no black could get
any part in our freckle-faced
strawberry blond cinema.

Young men looking to
find themselves and blood,
blood of my blood, young women
looking to be found. Where
was I for you.

Destroyed before we met.
You could not know that.
Why were you on the road too,
available. Road people are
usually losers or have dreams
and are trying to get away
from the death of staying home.
Your own mother and father destroy
you, no enemy, no stranger,
but the flesh that put you on earth.

I was violated in my boyhood
by the tip your forelock terror,
fear, my parents' fear of their jobs,
place in the community if any
child of theirs tried to become
a Poet or Ballerina or Actress.

Who did you think you were!
You ought to beg for a
file-clerk job in
the telephone company.

Screamed into you and
broke you, broke your heart
broke your ambitions, your
initiative and made you
overweight or in a hospital
or in drink.

The dead cannot regret
and a man like me
cannot either.

I was no one to go with
in the first place. But
once you came with me I
was no one to leave.

Freeloader of the sit-down girls who
do nothing. Who put out and go, flit
back and forth, never stay anywhere,
anybody's make. Lesbian meat too.
Before you are through you will be kept
by women once all the men are
wise to you and the hills of that
fantastic backside are starting to cave in.

Then a woman in bed on you or
you in bed on a woman will be better
than in darkness alone. You will
think of me then. You will often
think of me. I often thought of
you in cheap rooms when I had
no money and no woman.

I confess, I do not comprehend women.
They cling. All most men want is to
bust, feel good and be free. Women
know this, know they would be thrown out
until it was time to play with the
erector set again. The nest
builder has to capture a provider
or he'll seed her and be gone. I
have made few women happy long.
I make love to them and lose them.

The women who have known me, felt
the strong massage of my gripping
fingers manipulating their pimple-
speckled turkey carcasses best, can
say if I am more at home with men. You
will find me in a woman every time
you discover me in pitch dark, a
woman will be in my arms.

But do I ever really
remember the woman
for who she is or
only how I used her.

You fall in love with a good blow job.
The face of the lips gets to you. The
eyes looking up at you need to be told
you love them, and she does it so good she
wins your heart. Suddenly you want
all of her. You feel
you are going crazy.
It was so umcomplicated.
Now, where would you ever
find another woman who
would let you kill her
every day. You come to
think that she likes it.
Only it's crazy, she
leaves you.

She liked it. Nothing on
earth keeps doing what it
detests and she went down
right to it. She liked it,
or the only way to do what
you can't stand is to plunge
and get to it. Then, she
did it for fear of losing me
if she didn't. Imagine my
losing her.

Imagine! You left me in front
of the old Cafe Riviera, the
one Andy and Al ran in
New York City. You left me
drunk on the sidewalk. A man
you had held in your arms. You
left me drunk and mumbling,
realizing you were going. You
would not hear me beg you
not to leave me. You even
dressed up to say good-bye to me,
I remember how we were, how
poor we were, yet you managed
a cheap dress and high heels to say

good-bye to me. I had it coming.
But I wanted you. You were some
beautiful girl. You are as lost
as I am and you did the best
you could. You were wiling
to do anything with me to try
to find happiness yourself.

What can I say, I can't say
your name any more. I know
I had something when I was
with you.

I couldn't stop you from going.
I know the slobbering was an
act in my hooked cowardice of
how I expected I should look
like I was feeling about
your leaving me there on
the sidewalk in front of
everybody, when I was a
drunk gratefully relieved
of not having to cope with
you, the keeping of you
any more . . . wouldn't it be
nice to be able to rave
betrayed, betrayal from you.
You were untrustworthy.
No one knew where you were
liable to be or do, but
you betrayed no one. I
betrayed you. You stood me
past the limit of your
limited abilities.
You were yourself.

Blood of my heart, often I
will wake suddenly in the
night and see you coming to me.

Now here fitted together
the green window shade of our youth
is pulled down.

Water is falling on your grasp
off my brow.

But you will leave me and
years come I cannot forget you.

Love, my lover, why did you go,
why did you leave me so alone.
We were a pair.

Where will you be and will you
suddenly start, as a shadow in
the fallen evening hits your mirror,
makes your face drain ashen at that
moment realizing it took two people to part.

Across America the young boys
were let loose, when the niggers
stagnated in their juice for the
last time and the young yellows
poised to erupt on San Francisco
in the waning patience of the
young reds. Now the girls are
all emancipated. I wonder if they
will be any better to males, than
men have ever been to women.

The Whole Thing About Jedge's House

Across from the stadium in Jerome's cafeteria
we have just come from defacing monuments;
slurp our coffee feeling nervous
before taking the downtown train
to being nobody.

After the ball game, we walked jammed ramps
past bronze plaques to Gehrig,
Huggins and Jedge.
Sjome of us marked up their faces
in vicious compulsion
to cut down our betters,
our shoes covered
with the light orange cinders they walked in.

We said we loved them.
They look at us now scratched,
in the rain, in the sunlight.
Permanently mutilated
is our love for them.

We are the pot-bellied chuck-a-beers,
peanuts out of the shell in our rotten teeth,
with the foul stench
of gulped Hot Dogs on our breath.
Wounded animal whine from inside us rises
into shrieks over replanted
Kentucky bluegrass
like a huge card table with midgets.

Pitcher dealing from a huge
cut out of the green
to Catcher set for any action
like a Gunslinger.

In close Bagmen with a Shortstop to
pop the balloon of a hit.

Player comes to bat and as Pitcher moves,
mannequin triangle fielders fold

jackknife blades ready from a slingshot
to get that ball.

A Mantle is many things, a
Mantle is a cloak.
We can look at our sons remarking,
see, the old man
might have something left in him yet.

When Mickey hit he clobbered death.
Missing, his hand formed
as a Swan on a fishhook pulling greatness
vanished into the dugout again
in Jedge's house.

Staten Island Ferry

For a nickel the man
from the lower East Side
can ride the ocean.

Away from the skyline's
exhausted face, chiseled into
and blown apart for new
cheekbone features of glass buildings
rising above cold steel where
killers of people sprung from
the jobless traps, struggling
to take and rotting for it
in Attica.

The ocean-going liner
of people who have nothing.
Below decks on the long
rows of endless rigid
wood bench seats, poor
kids hug and tongue-kiss,
imagine! The only place
you have to try to make
love, a foul-smelling, dead-
cigar-stinking cold
Ferry boat.

The boy kid looks
like he's nothing
getting something.

As you walk by
the girl's big eyes
look apprehensive, but
her mouth is still on
his mouth, and he's
sprawled back with
his shirt loose out of
his trousers showing his
lean naked hard-muscled

wiry body, and he is
stiff down his left pant
leg, letting her work
herself up, like he's
out on his own private boat.

She makes you sense
that he's all she's got
and she's beside herself
trying to keep him,
even to letting the
public watch.

Filthy old sweaty boat,
sweat-encaked and hungry
Sea Gulls drilling the
Hudson of its refuse.

For a nickel you walk a deck
as though you can dream
you aren't a messenger and
don't pull a hand truck through thieves
grabbing a box out of your
too loosely tied hand truck load,
timed just as a bus stops and
the robber gets on and is
gone fast to his fence.

While you're trembling in gratitude
that he didn't knife or shoot you,
you're going to get home another
time tonight! . . . For a nickel out
on the Staten Island Ferry
you are rich, privileged to
go and come on the sea. Once
I knew a girl, beautiful like
a tulip, who climbed up in the cab
with the horny driver
and pulled his cord for him
that blew the whistle on them.

We had all been looking over
at Elizabeth, New Jersey,

when she honked our eyes
up to her wriggling around on his knees.

On our way to Staten Island, going
past the Lady from France, what
a dream! How easily man
forgets what he has
fought for and won, but
worse, his children,
not knowing what we went through,
give away the free breath we
got them with our lives. I love
you, lady with the torch and
all the corn that I believe in
because I like to go and come
as I please, unregimented and
without fear . . . like on the
Staten Island Ferry and off it
at my whim.

Staten Island, old graveyards,
back country roads so near the city,
and on the Staten Island Ferry a
feeling of reeling power that
a city should have such a
Ferry boat of Ellis Island dreams
after the big bridges, spanning
boroughs like a hand with
spread fingers on its wealth.

Yes, for a nickel anyone can feel
he has something that is his, alone.
For five cents you go on this boat out
across the harbor where
New York City stands at attention for you.

Helpless, We Go Into This Ground, Helpless

> Across the bridges and under the earth,
> subway trains lumber and clank.

Helpless, we go into this ground, helpless
each day packed against each other so that
we always start off irritable
at being tossed about thrown against strangers.

People who never get to know each other
but ride the train every day
without ever exchanging dreams.

> The subway screeches
> ear piercingly through tunnels
> and rattles into the station
> like an undone Accordion.

The whole subway train shudders
as it stops. The train doors
open like gasping mouths.

> And we get on staggering
> shadows of giants forced
> to become Subway Passengers
> pushing, shoving, we are made
> into something else than human
> in this insult cramming against each
> other in our own foul exhale.

> In the subway water
> always falling off
> station walls as though
> the held-back rivers
> will break through over us.

Here we are flushed out
of our anonymity.

> To whom do we look good?
> Villon, did you do that!

We get on the same train
every morning for years
and usually the same car.

                    Through the earth and on the bridges
                    subway trains groan. . . .

We get off the train
and go a hundred
different directions
to our daily fates.

We get on the same train
every morning, surviving
the subway each day as
prisoners do, disassociating
from what was . . . and is . . .
and will be . . .

                    But, Subways I
                    defeated you.

                    Overwhelming Subways I
                    hung on.

I climbed, climbed, climbed
your endless straight-up
stairs back out to sunshine.

Helpless, we go into this ground, helpless
onto dank dark brutally cold
impartial platform to wait
for trains that throw our insides around
until panic seizes and you gasp
in terror that you might suffocate,
with the scribblings of restrained
psychotics on everything, the walls, posts,
train windows, all over the trains in
insulting thumb noses at us vulgar orange, purple
which the rest of unstable us who somehow
cope must add to what we endure. We
let them draw on us rather than slaughter us.

But there is no such help for us,
if we suddenly blow it's Bellevue

or one of those unfortunate assassinations
by the good-guy off-duty cop who just happened
to be on his way home with a well-loaded gun ready
for us because we aren't ghetto kids
in the amnesty of invisible veiled threat to
go wild in our condition.

We go helpless down into this ground, helpless,
can you imagine getting stalled underground,
the subway train coming to a full stop down
deep in the earth in ninety-nine-degree heat,
the train stops and the sickening
scent of burning wood . . .

      Off the bridges and into the earth
      gouged out for it the subway train stalls.

Helpless, down in the ground, we are under
the earth now in company of people we don't
know . . . helpless into this ground, helpless.

We have resigned ourselves wrecks to them
these shattering, jarring subway trains that
we must take or not go anywhere.

Violent Dying

In Thanksgiving week of a cold poverty year
two men came in to rob a bar and
the gunman shot everybody.

New York, for you to let death loose
like this! New York what have you become
that you have a sewer smell of death.

New York, green in its dirt.
East River already floating dead to the sea.
And the Hudson dying of garbage
at our lady in the harbor's feet.

You are a thousand simultaneous actions,
in my system unlike the frighteningly
ordered cities, like a charwoman's best effort.

Humanity rushing up the underlining
of your belly to be spit out at their doors.

Starving men look bewildered
at High Rises across from their hunger.

A doormat is liable to be a human being
down at the bottom of the doorsteps of dying
in Manhattan, in New York.

You are a city where
a man could kill himself and lie dead
until he exploded through his orifices
and his blood fall down on his neighbors
not knowing what agency to call.

New York, weren't you my lover, New York?
Weren't you!? Didn't you take me into
your arms? Weren't we hungry together.

Do you kill your lover grown old,
a little gray and fat, but look in my eyes.
They are the cold steel of two bulls
that have put horns in all the matadors.

And I made you scream once and then die.
When you woke up I was gone. Now I will
not come to you again because if I do
you will kill me.

Death in your doorways, death
across the street exploding and blowing
heads off, death a little tiny blade
slipping into ribs, death
with the sour smell of burnt powder.

We are helpless in blinding sunlight
now in you, New York.

Your shadows are full
of merciless slaughter.

Who stops plunging the blade to
ask if you are Einstein! Who stops
if you are, who stops simply because
you are another human being who
does not wish to be struck down.

Death did not always seem to hover
on us. There were years some vague
world war one veteran uncle, your
mother's brother, stuck away in a
perpetual bathrobe always over his
beer and cribbage, that the family
whispered was mustard gassed, who
always looked at you through the
thick bifocals of his great injury,
was the only thing about death
you knew; your skin crawled around
him who had left his Altar Boy blessing
himself at all the Thou Shall Not Kill
masses, to kneel and receive communion
on his tongue before Infantry charges,
it seemed with God's blessing, while
he shoved his bayonet into man stomachs
and sudden frightened surprise blew
life out of those eyes as he followed
each bayonet plunge by pulling the

trigger and then forward and forward and
Oh My God I Am Heartily Sorry For Having
Offended Thee and then all the
world in his own ears.

How do you tell a lovely girl you
want to marry you that you kill
easily crossing yourself, blessing
it away, running with a herd of killers
with the wafer of God still dissolving.

New York death is
all over you.

Death is on your tall buildings
and death is in the streets.

The air we breathe
death.

Death now not death that
kills children who run in front of cars.

Death, murder, New York and I cannot
come in to you to be killed.

The Red Knight could go to him
jaunty with a flair and scarf
aimlessly in flames, but death
should not be for people come
into a bar to have drinks and birthday cake.

A girl turning thirty-nine reluctantly, bought
birthday cake to bring in to shake
routines, not to die.

Common, bars crowded with desperate
victims of the Manhattan trap, cold,
roach-filled apartment off hallways stenched
with the urine of a hundred years.

Despair drives the young who do not
grasp full meanings and penalties to
use up their own lives.

Because when you walk in and shoot everybody
you're going away forever.

Two men come in to rob and the
gunman shot everybody.

His companion begged him not to but
death had climbed into his skin, who
was no longer the old death of chivalry
you had to go find, but a
life seeker and a life taker.

The other man covering all of them in the bar;
How terror clutched them as they
dreaded, hoped and dared not move.

I know that professional killers can't
fleece you if you're dead, but only pick
your cold pockets, I know their butchers
get obliterated, Joe Jelly, who would corner
you and enjoy your helpless wriggling to live
as he put on white dress gloves and told you
that if you were nice and didn't resist he'd
put a quick one in your heart, but if you
gave him trouble he'd kill you slow,
so you'd roll around and think about it.

This gunman's companion begged him not to flash
death around like that, but he did not
shoot him to stop him, although murderer either way.

He didn't point his weapon at him and command
that they call the whole thing off or take the
money but call off death. No, he stood there begging
his companion not to do it but let him do it.

And murder was inside
the gunman's trigger finger.

He could be any of our sons, there are no
heroes home from wars these days.

What death can do to a man
to make him a killer of life
that never did a thing to him.

Killer, did you go over to war decent, but
they cut off ears in front of your eyes, they
wanted your insides cold to screams. They
brought out a beautiful young girl, tied her
between poles and made you watch them
pour gas on her and light it.

How could you come home and tell us that
we had violated you, taken away joy
from you forever.

How could you ever again be with a woman
without seeing her ablaze, your
children without ears.

So, you just walked into a bar
and the hunting license
is out on us all now.

I can no longer come into New York
out of my Connecticut cocoon.

If I sneeze and quickly reach
into my trenchcoat for kleenex
a thousand police guns will kill me.
They will have heard the bark of my nose
and my dying ears will hear their guns explode.

Good-bye, New York, New York of Hart Crane and
William Packard, New York of Garcia Lorca, New
York of Allen Planz. New York of my young manhood
held in your hand and blown over your harbors of
polluted death, good-bye greatest of the world's
cities, good-bye, I love you but good-bye.

Autumn

Brown, brown leaves,
brown strangled orange.
Brown orange stiff turned in cold air
to crumble and disappear.
Cider scent on the wind
blowing its breath on mud ruts
into congealed reflections
holding summer for a look.

Crossing America

This poem is for the woman
　　who crossed America with me

I

We hitchhiked America. I
still think of her.

I walk the old streets thinking I
see her, but never.

New buildings have gone up.
The bartenders who poured roses
into our glasses are gone.
We are erased.

II

Minook, Illinois,
one street out of nowhere through cornstalks.
Winter clutched the cornfields into Chicago.
Cold, we couldn't get in out of the cold.

But a lonely filling station owner risked
letting his death in out of the night.
I lay on his gas station floor and let her
use me for a bed.

I will never forget the cold into
my kidneys or lying awake bearing the
pain while she slept like a two month
old child on the hill of its mother's tit.

It was on that stone floor
that I knew I loved her.

III

Vermont, green, thick rich light
green and black green, green and
yellow Vermont, quiet, so beautiful,
but I fear your silence in narrow men.

So green. Green of death. Green murder.
Ruthlessness in green. The broken weak
whimpering among thick green meadows.
The oblivious green of love of the mountains

and lovers in each other, oblivious, and
you go to Frost's, now picnic tables
along the edge of the hideout.

Frost lived in green. 125 through Vermont
is a sliver thin line along thick rugged
country woods to the left, and across green
pasture green hills on the right with a
downhill mountain stream smacking clearly
off thick rocks almost to Middlebury.

Suddenly you're almost past it, just a
trail up through thick woods to the cleared
meadow and small white farm. Now the sky here
sits down on the roof to frame greatness burst
once out of that silence most of us couldn't
live long in, mosquitoes in thick heat lazy
summer and brutal winter that would drive us
mad in its isolation, yet it's no time at all
to the college or hardly a walk to Bread Loaf School.

This Frost's base, nothing could ever
get worse in life than this, brutal
cold on top of hunger, thick heavy
vicious snow and stifling heat summers
in a paranoia of green in silence green,
nothing harder; beat this and you've won
where Frost spent his years up a dirt road
in a small farm house with a barn that
had pulled its last winter when I saw it.

This maybe was his greatness to be able to
pull time but create, to be able to
lose everything but keep your grip and
create, the sustained self control and
inner will to live your years slowly through
green, thick green woods, dark rich green,
black green trees and green mountains and
the yellow dandelion green of highway 100
up over the ski green mountains where
the measles of yellow dandelions flush green
meadows in May, and I saw this Frost

country, it suited him, it was just like
him. You live like who you are in this green.

Frost lived in blood spouting green
and white blinding snow and was
stronger than anything that could
kill him, but finally death yanking him out
of the world he would not have ever left.

Green Vermont, green squeezing on
pressing green into bright spurting
red blood if you look. Green of the
mountains and the foothills and green
of the human spirit. You die in green
or you live in green . . . . It is in you
what you do.

IV

Cold, light off the road. Wreck of
a stranded car in the yard. Climbed in
thinking within, we could wrap ourselves
against cold cutting our livers
with its fingernails.

I went to the lit house fearing shotgun flash,
but there was no heat in the house either.
In a shack off the road a woman let me in
out of the brutal cold. She hovered with
eight children everywhichway on their one bed.

She let me in from freezing but she got up
and sat in a rocking chair and kept me
talking all night.

On the one hand she couldn't bring herself
to let me freeze outdoors and at the same time
didn't dare to trust me with closed eyes.

I knew she could kill me. I am alive
because I have recognized
death very close.

Where was the father of eight children
on this cold night.

I can see him, scrawny neck hunched over
steering wheel of a huge trailer truck,
maybe climbing Deer Lodge, Montana mountain
with his false teeth on the seat beside him,
tired and thin and not for long over the road.
I know him. He has given us a ride.

I told her my lady was cold in the wreck
but in that smug way one presumes that another
deserves what they get for being damn fool
to go traipsing with some idiot man
through the back washes of a continent,
she simply would not let her in out of the cold.

I told her our trip. She didn't
believe me. No one just comes to your house
who really has done all these things!
Both of us were relieved when morning broke.
She carried my death with her
right to the door if I wanted it.

V

On the highway to Vegas,
winter in your nose.
Off the road birds of death men
hovering over fires like icicles
thawing over a matchbook.
Snow over the pass. It was
no place for a young dumbbell.
These were numbered men
looking for fresh youth to turn over
like Indians surrounded deer
their deaths decided without
moving the wind. I turned back.

VI

The trick is to spot a
drunk who is well known in a

neighborhood bar and sit down
next to him as if you're life
long friends. You try to get him
to let you buy him a drink
effortlessly as if his letting you
is the most natural thing in the
world, you know each other so well
and you hope to be able to motion
the bartender up in front of the
two of you so he sees what appears
to be how close friends you are,
then it's just a matter of your
victim's ordering you a drink back,
20s, 10s, 5s, 1s up on the bar
loosely pushed so bartender can deduct
what he wants, and do not be a fool, be aware
that some drinkers are razor observant.
They couldn't walk, speak, but you move toward
their money and they see it and you're through.

VII

You've got to work smooth without
compunction, you're a drunk yourself
with a woman to keep, hardly able to
get in her, but you want to, you love
her, the liquor's got your lust, you
hope your girl doesn't get it
and go for a stallion, you're out
of your pimple facing San Quentin,
losing her if she gets wise to
the truth that you can't pop her
light bulb any more, only try
to feed you both.

Will she find out and go!? Steal,
loose cash on the bar in one movement,
then back to her you crossed the
country with, you want to drop
on your knees and lick her with love,
she's your woman and she won't stay

if she knows how you bring in
bus tickets to your new places.

You workin' other drunks
because you're grabbed.

Talent that might have run corporations
is fleecing drunks.

VIII

Young man has stepped out
of a cab and has helped the
girl out and now he has money
in his hand and just exactly
when he is being handed his
change and mentally is about
to tip the driver with
plans to turn and tip the
doorman and then the
waiter, while he's in this
frame of mind, turning now
from the cab to tip the doorman,
you step in from nowhere fast
and right next to him, but
loud enough so he sees the girl hear
you, you stem. You bum him and get
out of there before the doorman realizes it.

IX

He sat down next to a
Merchant Marine Officer who
just spent the afternoon of
his first day ashore in months
sodomizing and beating up a
fourteen year old girl hustler
off the Embarcadero, but now would
self-righteously gouge out
the eyes of anyone who tried
for his money up on the bar,
although were he suddenly yanked

to police station, with the chicken
pointing him out, he'd be begging
for compassion if not outright
understanding, everyone's
insight comprehending him, you know
the type, goes around telling
everyone his name's Tokyo, heavily
tattooed and seething restrained
danger. He rushes to sea when
he can't keep it together on land.

X

And your car standing on its hind legs up
the Pulaski Skyway or blinking through sweat
shivering heat on the New Jersey Turnpike,
amid the big oil drums by Hoboken when you
come from Harrison in ninety-nine degree heat
to drive into the darkness of the Lincoln Tunnel
or go onto the race track of George Washington
Bridge over into the city of the score, New York,
strained now so your instinct tells you it is like
a hard boiled egg shell about to be cracked
for the dried yellow . . .

America, you built too fast, rushed inside
two hundred years instead of centuries
Europe took, and China put lime over its cultures
so many times, this world can never know
what it lost.

Garcia Lorca sing!
Where that inebriated Hudson vomits.
Sing of green for me
who has seen the Spanish boys hang in Riker's Island
convicted of no crime, but without
bail money, take their
own lives in humiliation.

You and I are bitter together, Federico!
At the death of these roses.
Blood red they die,

blood of the immigrant
who lands without the new language yet,
handicapped and always
at the bottom of Commerce,
the end of reward, the chance
they took! It is from these, Federico,
that America was put together, blood
red they die, blood of the immigrant
at the feet of the statue of our lady
with her torch high in welcome
but cold stone of death.

Rain and the sea
splash her with the slush
of wild snow storms and
reveal her inner hardness.
She is an immigrant herself
given as a gift.

Though she welcomes, you
have to bring your own money
or find it without getting caught or
she will let you toss and turn in Hell.

Across from her open palms
lie cell blocks of despair.

Mark us our Bicentennial then with
their bones, for they came to blend
their hearts and all their effort too
in our dream. Who among us has
not stolen. Who among us does not
kill everyone they live with in order
to be whatever their dreams
are, come on! Federico,
you died because your ego thought
you were God but you forgot He
was sent to Heaven.

Come on Federico! we must not
mark our Bicentennial
until no man can languish

or die imprisoned in a land
of the free and brave.

Until no man hangs himself
because he has no hope.

That day my bitterness, Federico,
will concentrate itself completely
on your murderers.

It is a world again now
of torture and violation.

Yes, I will see this, Federico, yes,
see it and rage against it.

XI

Walt Whitman, because our whole song
springs from the nest of your whiskers, I
scream to you of poor people, scream Walt! We
go to the moon, but still children are
hungry, still infants have no father
and mother and are left newborn healthy
beautifully formed, born alive, in plastic
bags to die like that behind Finasts . . .
murdered children, abused children! Hungry
children, children are hungry and full of
rickets in your country, Walter.

Allen Ginsberg, what on earth is Gertrude Stein
doing to you down in your Cherry Valley . . .

Hart Crane, while you were noting
the telephone poles stretching across our ghost . . .

Violence, eye gouging out horror is easy.
Bullets end you at once, life takes
a long time to make, an instant to obliterate.
Forever, virginity goes forever in one
plunge . . . and your car
one dizzy speeding uncontrolled dot trying
to find the whole world's heart . . . and your car

standing on its hind legs up on the Pulaski Skyway . . .
as mankind crashes head on . . .

XII

I have called the frogs
in from croaking in bogs, now
that their timeless complaint,
along with blinking fireflies,
in mortal man dark, is
lost in ascent to the stars
and I wonder how soul
will go to God
from such foreign place.

XIII

Now, outside that bus station was Cheyenne, see,
but I didn't go look. I was young and I'd be
back! What could it be but a city with buildings,
because I was on my way to the Dakotas, where I
never got, and the thing that hurts later is that
I was right there in Cheyenne and didn't stay
awhile and look around. I never got back there.
The bus we rode into Wyoming that time
when I was young pulled into the run down part
of town. Even the idea of days-old cellophane
wrapped sandwiches for sale in the dirty old
bus station of cows, revolted us. Somebody hanging
around the station, gawky with a blank face, said
that across the street from the station you could
get a real good steak. I really didn't believe it,
the place looked gray, but it was one of the best
steaks I ever ate anywhere, right across from the
old Cheyenne, Wyoming bus station.

XIV

Taos, old Taos of the trails, Taos, old
adobe, mud and water squeezed together through
your fingers by your human hand into

thousand year houses. We rushed to pick cabbages
out of the frost in a field of the William Hawk
ranch high on a mountain of San Cristobal that
looked down across Comanche plains. Big bears and
Indians, a National Park now, not free any more,
not wild and forbidding. It doesn't stir your
blood any more. The outdoors is spoiled. Gone.
Gone the excitement of straw and mud and water
shoveling just dirt out of the ground, just dry
grass straw and then pouring water on the straw
and dirt, water on the dry straw and earth making
mud and then slowly kneading, squeezing them,
oozing them through your fingers again,
again until all the straw and mud mix and
become shaped by human hands to make a house
that in this dry hard country will last hundreds
of years, wild country, cold in the morning and
clean sharp air cold in loneliness and guitar strums.
The horses were so wild and so lovely, so beautiful
wild horses. You can make love in the cool dark adobe
mud and straw and water where Kit Carson stayed
in the old old hotel of Taos square. . . . It is amazing
but when you put that straw water and mud together
the weather outside can be dry 100 degrees hot and dry
yet inside the adobe room is damp and cool and here
the Spanish, Navajos, Pueblos. . . . Ceremony of killing
pig in front of everyone hanging the big poor
squealing thing upside down and then razor sharp
slitting its throat, everyone watching, everyone gathers
and watches the throat slitting like a Catholic ritual,
then everyone gets a piece of the death according to
their importance, hard ruthless country, the really
ageless America getting ruined by rancid tourist
gas on the arroyo.

XV

Sheriff of Oxford, Mississippi wouldn't
give us a bed unless we committed a crime.
But the wife of a hard hotel owner let us
leave our luggage for sleep. A car stopped

to my thumb but when I grabbed the door an
electric jolt hit me. An Oxford priest gave
us money. I even forget his face and never
got it back to him. On the back of a pick-up
truck, bouncing around straw as he drove fast
through Tennessee murdering me as much as he
dared, and my lady up in his cab while
he weighed our lives with his gas pedal
foot and whether to take her and dump me.

XVI

We made love in the breeze of the Gulf. I
loved her. It was like loving myself. I
wanted no one else; I murdered a catfish
with an ice pick in the kitchen of our
apartment, carried him up betrayed
in a pail of salt water. Reached in and
grabbed him thrashing as I stabbed him
with the ice pick, flailing the sea in my
ears; trying to throw himself out of my grip
back to the ocean. My hand kept driving
the ice pick through him into
chrome sink until the heart of
his life gave itself to the ice pick.

XVII

In the night our black friend
would sneak to our door in stocking feet,
we'd pull curtains because he told us
we had to if we wanted him alive.

He did not think I would ever come
to his house. I saw what we white men
will pay for in Hell. Children, the
terror of my presence in their eyes.

They were in the living dead part of town
where men plunge themselves furiously
into women rather than kill somebody.
Faces of infants are old.

Nigger, your blood
in the daisies of Gettysburg, your
grave out back of some cesspool.

XVIII

No, not again in the night,
terror and us in camps.
I am in the woods alone with you
Red Robin. Hear the bulldozers
shaving our forest away for a drive-in,
death is waiting where delicate freedom
bloomed. Open space keeps screams futile.

Stop it now! Stop even the idea, the chance,
camps again, a Borman out
of the jungle into the White House
with a paint job of blood.

What was the immigrant that his own children
cut open earth of his grave
and wet dust of his bones
with innocent blood of his own kind!

XIX

You are gone like buffalo never
existed in my time, except up from Pueblo,
Colorado, a freak herd for truck diner
steaks now. In a museum for children
who will never know they roamed
open plains as you whistled on a halo
of congealed smoke through quiet
back-o-towns pulling our nation together
like a stubborn zipper on the trousers
of an Aldeman, Choo-Choo, I rode your
passenger cars bursting with pride
at the trail you cut in the face of cliffs
and rock slides where snow and ice owned
the country until you charged through
on tracks put down by expendables of mankind,

buying their progeny piece of America
with their bare tendons and their deaths.

I did not miss you until you were gone.
We are in a skyspin now. The shadows of
space fall on your ghost.

XX

The apple country when
Sunday smelled of our taste buds,
our loneliness rattled in freight
eluding irises of law men, north
to apple picking and then to pick vines.
There is nothing so wrong as steel bars
on wide open land like daggers in
innocence, a life of jails, camaraderie
with sheriffs tolerantly turning the key
on our weekends because we were not
prison time, but to be yanked out of sight
once our power was in tavern cash registers
and our anguish blew up in the drink.
Staggering behind Sally Tambourines
down your main street. All you saw
was your flag, never the wrecks of men
who were broken in your service or
shook Mamma loose, scattered in
Father dictum "if you do this
you are on your own."

XXI

Friday night in Colorado towns
helping the sheriff make his count,
he'd work with you all week if you
helped him look ridding the community
of vagrancy and bums when the good
working voters come out to drink
and spend their futility on
draining beers and didn't want
to stagger against indigents.

So into a cell with the door left
wide open unlocked, as long as
they were off the street, out
of the way provided with cigars
and cards and a chance to read
the papers, rest up for your time
on the town, when Monday morning
came again and none of the
sheriff's men would do a thing
about your bumming people on
the street, no matter how many
complained, nor would the
sheriff's deputies do a thing
about your even falling down
drunk of heat any other day
of the week, as long as you didn't
fall head first through any windows
or knife anyone or do anything
you shouldn't.

XXII

Now flash to Reno on speed highways
by old Donner Pass road hidden now
like a hunched shoulder you felt like
you'd drive right off into the postcard.

Cold, with tree scents on clean ice air,
everything so thin, small, saddle leather
and rancid gun scent, horse flesh smell like
the taste of fresh rhubarb in your nose, and
surrounded by a vast world, yet impeded by
only your two feet, horses, you could die
inches from where you started in snow chomping
on your neighbor's chest meat that thrust
itself out from Missouri across this land
with just one more mountain to get over
to the ocean . . .

XXIII

We crossed Southwest with a nurse
driving herself to Pittsburgh, haunted
loneliness in black quiet night giving
dying cigarettes a free ride too hanging
in ashes on her lower lip, she plucked
us off L.A. Freeway concrete and you
had the feeling you were riding with
one of those men women who rode
with George Patton, now forced against
her will to take leave from completely
taking over and bullying frail old
people in some Los Angeles home out at
the edge of death. She took us
away from hovering arresting
police roaming in cars to put
hitchhikers in jail and out she
drove, no one talking, in the love
of midnight, when there is a
truce with silence, out into the
desert across Arizona and Texas to Galveston.

XXIV

It was just around the corner from night.
The town was a half block stuck in the middle of cornstalks.
And in daylight heat wrung your breath
until strangers separated like chaff dropped over.

Early morning just touched blackness now,
but it was as if the town knew I was there and
turned on all its lights. Sun exploded
on long green fields with yellow corn peeking.

A dog barked in a house at my unknown scent. It was then
I sat on the seat of my suitcase and wrote you a postcard,
feeling I bought my living as it slipped into the mailbox
as human beings started moving about me like a decided jury.
The town came out to see me in pairs of overalled men,
resentment in their eyes and I sat down in their diner over coffee

absolutely terrified and the coffee turned into ham and eggs
to show solvency to their invisible rope.

It was a town behind me in the shifting of the next ride's gears
and we'd be in miles of fields of corn, yellow through green.
But now I hovered on the whim of human frailty
where all my knowledge might not mean anything.

XXV

It was not all right with her,
the lying together times.
She wanted me to come
to the town of her doll house
and ask her.

Self-righteously I fumed.
The air blew up in my curses.

How could a woman travel with you
and ask you to come and
ask her . . .

XXVI

My father was tired and old
when I came bulbously demanding
the rest of his squeezed out dreams,
shattered enough before I was thrown
by him one night into my mother's eggs.

I know he loved himself,
so me as part of his flesh,
but we were as removed
as lovers as soon
as the screams have died.

He tried to buy Heaven
by giving me pocket money.

We could never get our love out
across the veil of my dead mother.

We asked him where we would live
when the cover came down on her coffin.
"Here, this is your home" and
it always was.

For all the years unable to cope I
write this, for all the ruined children
of others pacing their lives out in white
rooms I write this, stab me with thorns
of roses for writing this, let ground glass
be in all I eat for the loathsome back handed
ingrate treachery of writing this, but youth
does not cut its trail on the whim of the old man.

XXVII

All the daddy are deep in the ground rotting,
while what they produced are racing to rot
on the earth soon. There is no forgiveness when
·you ruin a child, not even if the child forgives you.

If he had been a simple dishwasher
he would have had a father.

"He aren't one-a-them homasoxuals, th'po'try's
just a hobby," Dad rushed to assure th'Maine folk
leaving him out of his heart
in the cold of his fidgety disgrace.
Presume dad was mortified because he wasn't
discussing my crushing shoulder bones
on a football field, bouncing balls in a track
suit or digging spikes into somebody's ankle,
all the pursuits for your son if it wasn't
hunting season when a'course any real boy'd
wanta be out wind blown rosy cheeked blowin'
birds apart or bringin' down a deer just
because it was November when you bring deer down,
certainly not for need of meat.

That he could have lived to see me
finally tall in his place, with his last name
proudly on everybody's lips.

XXVIII

Ten miles into
Chicago, what legs
my lady has.
Powerhouses throb
in her calves.
Her swaying backside
thumbs itself
at the highway.
We do not lie
in one of its ditches.

XXIX

There was a woman who was
on the bum who must have
worn eleven dresses and she
always carried a shopping bag
that she lived out of and in a
couple of the bars they let her
buy drinks of wine if she had
money or they let anyone buy
her a drink and he would sit
there sipping thirty cent shots
with a fifteen cent ale chaser,
buying her doubles of wine, week
after week, day after
day of coming in from stemming.
Good stemming days he'd have
given the bartender money, always
trying to keep at least ten dollars
back of the bar and he made friends
with pensioners and other bums
so they always tried to see to it
that each other always drank.
He was a young man sitting with old
men in bars rather than an old man
sitting with young men in the bar and
often when he was leaving, Alice,
the woman in eleven dresses with

that fresh air encaked smell on her
would walk with him, carrying her
bag with whatever she owned and
whatever she'd been able to grab in
it and on occasion he'd let her
come up into his hotel room and
let her fall down on the warm floor
in out of the outdoors night cold
with the rug of the floor over her.

He'd offer her the bed and she'd
refuse, so there would be the two
of them, him stripped to his shorts
lying sprawled across his bed
bought by a quick odd job or from stemming,
sleeping his drunk off while she
passed out on the floor. Finally he
was there with her and the urges
of a man hit him fiercely. It was
about the end of his being down,
blood flowed through the cold pipes.

But she had morals or her feelings
were wrung out or in her position
she couldn't have it around that
she'd make or everybody'd pass
her from bum to bum or the
police would send her over, but
he put it to her like a bastard
that he'd been buying her drinks
and food for three months and
when he actually got so low
as to put it to her that way
she got up off the floor and lay
on her back on the bed and
the smell of her from exposure
to outdoors almost made him
vomit, it was like blood on tin
on the roof of your mouth, but
he plunged in her like he was
murdering her cunt and he
was so hard from lack of it

that after awhile a spark from
somewhere way in her moved her,
still she just lay there while
he screwed his drinks back.

Until he burst and then he held her
in his arms close and her face
underneath him looked like wax
death smelling vile wholesomeness
of fresh wind and outdoor sun turned
like milk left out on a stove, then
he held her in his arms and even
while he was doing it fear crossed
his soul at the thought that he was
laying death, that the time he met
his death it would be Alice in
eleven dressed pulled up so her
hole could be entered only he
wouldn't be pulling out . . . and
he put it in her all night like
a drunken lottery ticket winner.
She just lay there smelling cold
like death would smell if it
was a woman with a hole.

In her and holding her and
back and forth until he had
come and until he had come
then she got up off the bed
without a word and picked up
her shopping bag and left.

He never forgot her. The face
when he lay over her, death
letting him know what she
will look like when she comes
for him.

He regretted his drunken insanity
almost as soon as his cock lay
whimpering in its shriveled
case and tried to talk to her
but she hadn't given herself

to him. He had put it to her
that really all the drinks he
bought her weren't for human
friendship, but for this. He
was right and she was right.

XXX

She walked out of his room
at four in the morning, nothing
he could say would stop her. Fear
seized him then that the police
might grab her for wandering
around that hour of the morning
and find her reeking of sperm and
come get him with a rape rap,
but the night passed and they
didn't come.

She never spoke to him again
and she never came into the
bar any more. She never saw
him again. Under the grime
encaked dirt he guessed she
was still under forty. What
had brought her down?

She still had the human spirit
to give him his sex when
he put it to her that this
was, apparently, the only reason
he'd ever sat with her, ever
bought her a drink, ever
had anything to do with her.

He never saw her again and
he never got rid of that smell
about her of cleanliness gone sour
from too much outdoors.

Massachusetts Poems

Meeting Richard Wilbur

Leaves of life ago
I climbed stairs at Wesleyan trying
to look expected. No one took me for a student.
Afraid I'd be asked what I wanted, I walked
around first, staling the air with smell of fright.
When I intruded, kindness asked me in.
My eyes drew the room. Luck found a vase
for me to look like I was looking at,
something we could pretend I noticed . . . . would he
see me unaccomplished, shout me out the door? No.

Few know a Ming vase and I didn't, so
taking professor's delight
in curiosity, Wilbur told me it was one.

Boston

Boston is what we imagine, memories
Breed's prejudice hill, Ann
Hibbins throttled from great Boston Common Elm
legs thrashing the air trying to outrun rope's snap.

Indians, great building climbers
who were dying in deprivation
in isolated bars. You'll be sitting drinking
when a couple of stools down from you weapons

will show the blinding yellow moon
in their sinking blades. But even if
it's happening to a Warrior you
were just discussing building climbing with

you don't move. They understand you're
man enough, but though living in
your culture, the very Indian you'd help
who may have yellow moonbeams through

his liver will let out the red of the roses of you,
living in your life angry you don't understand his,
but nothing will touch you if you don't disrupt.
The Irish have climbed to be shot down

for committing the worst mortal sin, ignorance.
Jews are fragile in our guilt. North End
looks washed and vanished, no overturned
garbage can puke. If you disgust Italians

they'll stuff a drain pipe with you. Blacks, in
the heartbreak of visibility, wreck litter
broken glass filth, raped by us turned loose
chattel without our good wishes to die we hope.

Among us smirking disturbed beneficiary
of special attitudes, relaxed rules, feeling it
hopeless, then hateful . . . Boston, salesmen,
racetrack action, food while Mamma

and the infants are left peering out windows
of mortgaged house on the green street

lucky to eat Chili, while you're eating in dining rooms,
"What'll you have th' Lamb Chops?". . . . time to

go with Ms. who understands you knows real you
in crazy wonderful Boston, Boston's
th' life, Bird, Yaz
a whole menu.

Downtown has turned traffic around one way so you
can't drive through Chinatown up by the big stores any more.
Around us 128 is bent like a spread bow skeleton
to sling us into New Hampshire and Rhode Island.

Visiting Emily Dickinson's Grave

Where else would we go first in Amherst!
But no one is in the graveyard tilting
stone sinking chiseled letters fading.

All around streets flood Autumn "Leaf Peepers" come
to watch great umbrella blush through green
mixed yellow in pumpkin.

It is a rough skuffy day of dirt picked
by the wind and thrown. The town is
packed for tag sale downtown

three blocks from the grave but no one
visits you placed like a greeting hostess
across from a garage

that looks in its oil
by filling pumps like a
massacre of serenity, rather

than with your back to Amherst
so you could always see your big red brick house,
who is coming and going.

Along motel route over from Northampton
"No Vacancy" signs show how full of people
Amherst is when the year puts on its colors.

But no one in the graveyard, not
even any flowers, no flag either
or Perpetual Flame.

What Can I Leave for You to Feel of Me

Up Mohawk trail beautiful peaceful green
and then Taconic forest white birches clinging
to hills like hands of skeletons jammed
together, they have all come home from everywhere a
birch tree ever was and here they are
astounding on eye sight but when not in
green leaf, like some kind of stark white alive death.
Back down green mountain unfolds a meadow town,
on top of snow the very wind is Indians, Caghnawagas,
Abenakis, from Loretto, Huron led by Thaouvenhosen,
come on the fierce wild wind packed snow higher
than Palisade wall to hatchet Sheldon's door
of heavy plank double thickness, kill Deerfield,
carrying captives into Vermont up White River
over mountains across short divide to
headwaters of Winooski downstream to
Lake Champlain into Canada, slaughtering
those who couldn't keep up on the way and in
Canada to be butchered, burned alive or ransomed.
Now, thinking of it, thinking, say, of Sheldon's
Deerfield, Massachusetts door before you see
it, hatchet cracks like sunburn peeling flesh
hacked into the door hanging, but now the fury
is only a hole. Age makes old wood smooth, the
death is vanished, but a chance to touch with
your own fingers, if you believe it's really the door,
the door got away to Rhode Island for awhile, is this it?

If you believe it's really the door, to touch the same door
another man cut furiously through years ago to
prove word of mouth in books true. Look!
Here is the very hole all right a rifle fit through
and shot wild killing a woman starting to get up off
her bed in an instinct sensing immediate fatal
danger that was the surest intuition she ever had.
What can I leave for you to feel of me.

Four Short Poems

Through the World the Little Worm Forever

In blizzard at toll booth
trucks backed up like
empty egg crates, their
lights on in the snow falling linen dust
makes them look furious beetles,
bright round large bulbous glazed eyes
dead or glaring, like giants
tied held prisoner, taunted,
by something that didn't occur to them possible.

All backed up the falling snow
flicked against trucks windshield glass
like feathers of cotton candy sticking
to windows like furry little hands it
takes scraping to get off. Cold sticking
and cunningly worked under their
big thick tires to skid them out of control.
Through the world the little worm forever while
big species vanish, invisibility is power,
victory your opponent's ignorance.

Boxing

He'd snap his right up
to smash cheek while it
was his left to the jaw nerve
like the Asp's tongue, one dart;
and to take him all you had to
do was trip his rhythm, change
his feet movement any way
you could, stamp on the floor,
duck, any way. . . . you change the
feet and his plan was gone. You
had him. But you had to step in
and do it! I seen one time a
guy hesitate after throwing him
off good and it was over.

The Assassin

I am hidden within
who you think I am.

Schwartz, in Three Words, Delmore, You Said "Keep Your Head"

You are insight we failed.
Our mind missed your grasp.

How brilliantly you express
where men begin not to be brothers.

And that our own words, our own reason
will tell us the Universe has not ended.

Even if we are in a sealed air tight dark box
and some voice calls to us, "The world is over!"

In our mentally realizing we were hearing
as we always had heard, reflecting the news,

Still breathing, our breath clutched in
anxiety as our locked in condition demanded;

as you put it, Delmore, in a tight situation
our mind would tell us things were the same,

nothing was through, but we might be
unless we outwit the voice that called to us,

"imagine" whatever the key is
to get out of the box,

defeat those whose plan conceives we'll try
to reason our lives and so survive.

New and Uncollected Poems

With Eberhart at Occom

That day Eberhart
must move a tree
out of the way. What it
must have done to him,
the stab of sorrow.

To kill a tree
when you have denied
yourself killing a devil.

We love Eberhart
for his kindness
to our frenzied image.

Trying to place
your car near Eberhart's
house that looks at
Vermont down a
banking of New Hampshire
across Connecticut river

was risking falling
off what ants
call a mountain top.

A great quilt of autumn
and Samson Occom
in the frosted colors of Dartmouth.

In this country the
trees blood green blushing
December snow.

Vicious teeth of a bulldozer
taking a tree by surprise
ripped out of the earth
as if no seed had ever
burst a root and grown
wide and tall with
branches and pine needles.

York, Maine

FOR THEODORE JUNKINS

Through the cutty Sark motel room 21 picture window now
the gray waves coming into York Beach like
an invasion of plows pushing snow. Tomorrow
the sun will scratch its chin and bleed along the skyline
but today everything is gray poached in a steam of fog.

Inedible Sea Gulls, domesticated by human charity,
obliviously peck the land sweeping around like a
sprung fish chowder of rocks of vanished summer
when the outsider empties his pockets here for relief,
fresh salt air, the silence, soothing asleep.

Junkins Country here up the old Berwick road 91
past Mcintyre Garrison built against Abinakis and
Moody's actual church used as a barn now. Junkinses
intermingled with Pines and this earth is Junkins earth.
The Junkinses are spread around the woods here

in little graveyards, beware of hunters if you
try to find their resting places. At Scotland Bridge road the
great stone arch with the name Junkins chiseled out of rock, an
arch of stone all by itself like an entrance to a great
castle but only to a mud rut farm house road with little boys

standing tall and ready to spring if they have to, looking curiously
at you by their swinging tire from a string wondering what
you see in piled rocks they see every day—hardly! Perhaps they
   do
know that Moody lies within steps of their yard, Moody of the
shooting accident so he did not wish to show his face to men
   again.
On a day like this the dead seem to appear. They
were here alright! Blue is overcome by gray
Sepia gray, Umber gray, raw Sienna, burnt Sienna.
Gray seems no color at all. You see it, but how
together? I can come to the under colors.

If I could find it, I could find the answer to life
to what to expect. God's energy, the day's changes,
clouds like a veil, and then the sky clear blue
as if this world has no other color, the sea
just exploding here.

Pulling Oar

Every January my hands
still blister, callous over as
they did each year I was number 4
of engine rooms, rowing's
power to throw Coxwains
overboard and take the shirts
home off backs of Crew fallen
exhausted over their oars like
stacked flat pancakes, beaten.
Fresh water, salt water, polluted
water, makes no difference; lakes,
rivers, bays, canals, irrigation
ditches, wherever there is enough
width, length. The water rowed on
effects how the race is rowed, how
boats are rigged but we'll row
anywhere any time sweating,
fearing "catching a crab" which
means the force of the boat moving
forward may cause the oar to turn
under water; in my sleep I dread
catching a crab a place like
Onodonga lake or even a smaller
Eastern Sprint like in Worcester.
Pulling oar, that lust, urge needed
to part water without speedboat blade, our
common secret wish to be the best
we can make ourselves . . . until,
in the sweat of stroke, we are
in it and the water
of our sweat is dropping
into the water of competition.
Everyone counts, every
stroke together, the
crackling ripple of our
shoulder muscles stops
the very wind's face as

we depend on correct rhythm
of our Cox's call; if she or he is
off at all it can kill the stroke
of our heart's attempt.

Ode to Karl Shapiro

Along the Hudson and Westchester
the lone heterosexual rides his last maiden
into her screaming dawn.

From now on she'll be known as all knowing
liberated woman who doesn't give anything to you,
and doesn't want anything.

Your size means nothing to her and
what you can do with it, nothing and
it means very little to her if she does it,
and very little if she doesn't.

The city of New York is cracked. Where the moon rises
Karl Shapiro lands at Idlewild. Along Broadway
Jack Dempsey's is become th' home of th' Whopper
and George M. Cohan finally looks ridiculous
in Pigeon expression.

From the jungles of the South Pacific pulling
detail on Pacific isles, came home Karl Shapiro
with Bill Mauldin and Ernie Pyle, everybody's
cartoonist, everybody's drinking buddy correspondent,
and a poet who was in a war.

Karl Shapiro home like the Lion of Judah on
the pages of the *New Yorker*, put a Pulitzer in
his pocket and to Chicago, edited, then
Japan, India, Germany, Nebraska . . . California.

Along the Hudson and Westchester the
highway broke apart and fell down on
pier scurrying thieves underneath.

The old west side trail crushed from
trucks, taxi cabs and motorists weaving
in and out in sudden death hurry.

Drenching the air in sweat and gas
while a thousand shady deals cost lives
and it cost your life to try and stay alive.

In the dawn moon the lone heterosexual
rides his last maiden singing "Hi-Ho
Blonde Chick aw-waay!" and swinging Edsel
landed at Kennedy.

Karl Shapiro, I sing to you from my youth for
your great courage when you didn't have to and
it would have profited you more not to stand up
against the WASP and the FASCIST.

But this will not be one-a' them revealing tributes,
in which I cry "This one, too, Karl, this one,
too, is a bisexual faggot under the skin!" . . . or
"Hey, Karl, bebbe, whachoo doin' down there
among th' Irish!?"

When this nobody came to you, you who were everything
embraced me. I have only imagined poems,
you, Karl, have written them.

What it was to read your images! Freeing us
from Whitman long before Allen told us it was
all right to tongue somebody's ear out, you wrote
"Buick" and "Nigger" while Federico saw
butterflies in Walt's beard and, excited,
a youngster, I wrote. . . .

TO BEGIN WITH

> But my years now
> in half seconds each squeezed for the utmost.
> Defeated House Invalid's complete ceasing.
> Fire the Pilot Light in the furnace of myself
> like one kneeling outdoors on a windy night
> presses lips close to the new starting fire,
> softly blows it to re-kindle where the spark had died.

And, swimming in my head your "Buick," Karl, I wrote then,

STAY LOOSE

When the rent man comes frothing into your pig-sty
eyes throwing you out, and the rat you've been sharing with
tip-toes cross door ledge behind him refusing to spring
bite into his roast beef fed neck that his face juts off

like a constipated owl as his drool hangs at the crevice
where a chin, somewhere in the rolls of greasy flesh should be,
ask him back. Be a host who's too busy to see a sick friend,
while his look pops disbelief as he can't catch his breath.
Push him back in that hall an animal would go blind in.
Gently slamming the door and bending, shove through
to his greedy little reach an envelope on which is scribbled,
small as a needle point . . . I'm moving . . . soon . . . soon.

Along the Hudson and Westchester
that road has broken off with us.

And downtown the chortling clowns
hustle us, Karl, out of our literature.

Second rate mediocrity arriving to read
what they call their "poems" on stages
like The New School, nasty mean people
always lugging knapsacks bent over like
the crawling things they are, struggling, not
about poetry but careers, what will be bad
enough not to threaten and so allowed.

There may be no Schliemann to find
the lost Troy of verse, Karl, and no
one who even knows Delmore Schwartz.
No one who reads Eberhart and Jarrell,
Allen's Kaddish or the Federico
Watermelon poem or who ever
heard of the Naome Replansky.

But, Karl Shapiro, I sing to you for standing
for these people and these things. I sing
to you for myself because you gave me
myself in my art and you gave me yourself.

Oscar Wilde Lament

I THE GRAVE OF OSCAR WILDE

You lie not in England but among the French,
the Epstein Winged Sphinx of your tomb desecrated.
Something gouged the penis and testicles of stone
off the Winged Sphinx. Is it your "exquisite grotesque
half woman, half animal" come in form of English lady
to be certain the stone Sphinx is female? As "she
who loved Anthony and painted pharaohs" reminds
you want "that rare young slave with his pomegranate
mouth," not look to tourists who parade Père Lachaise
like a flying stud leaping through stone to mount any
maiden from the dark earth. No, out of doom, out of
ages something has said "Forever!" to us, to Epstein's
soul, no, you cannot undo what the earth has taken.
Perhaps you wished you were a lover of women, but you
loved the chameleon and the snake with loins and
hurt blue eyes that show pain will snuff them out.
Something, someone who knew well your "bestial sense
that would make you what you would not be," in physical
form of English woman crossed the channel and cut
your stone Sphinx and the way the testicles and penis
are chipped like razor sharp chisel powerfully
driven makes you shudder seeing a Ripper murder
or an ageless female Sphinx you wrote about who will
not let any mortal make her into a man even in stone.
She rides you still who loved Anthony and saw time begin.

II READING, BERKS

Just over the wall
of your Reading prison where
you wrote for a man being hung

hanged Hugh Cook Farringdon, Catholic Abbott
where The Holy Brook of The Seven Rivers
of Reading ran

riches to threaten Henry the 8th's
throne, so he hanged
Hugh Farringdon

and now only the shell of ruined walls stands
soon to crumble and vanish forever,
just over the wall of Reading Gaol.

They have made the top
of the wall around Reading Gaol
round now

so that hooks of escape
cannot get a hold to lift
human spirit over.

And just over the wall of Reading Gaol
stands the biggest carved lion
of its kind in the world, yet

the lion's feet point the wrong way.
When this was pointed out to the artist
that no cat stands like that

he went and stood under
his work and
killed himself

where The Holy Brook
runs of The Seven Rivers
Of Reading. . . .

. . . And so you died
of a broken heart, Oscar, yearning for
Westminster Abbey, at least a plaque like
Auden, but he didn't go to prison; your
head cracked by a guard's club in Reading Gaol,
shattering your hearing and your life young
to stumble Paris only a short while far away
from Frank Miles now and the culture your
wit sent chuckling from bedroom, theatre, cricket match.

Motel

I

We came in off the Parkway past two
union pickets silent in their shivering behind
signs since Reagan and The Air Transporters.

This is a new one from the most famous luxury chain,
just opened, with a special cheap rate to fill
rooms and give staff practice . . . that

succeeds because the help's picked from immigrants.
Cocktail waitress forced to wear outfit that
makes her look stripped, fired if they catch

her chewing on her mouth looking like it's got
anything in it but her tongue. Athletic teams,
Corporations hoping that false front if not their

products gets business will fill this place,
depression outside or not. Starving human
beings within a mile or not.

Poverty is within walking distance of this place
up little oil dirty snow side streets here. Hunger
shows in the punctured tattered half drawn

window shades and in the cold pipes without heat.
Murder just to eat and for something warm, a scarf to
clutch around your adam's apple and try not to

think of the numbness of the rest of your body
lonely so cold, to control rage at being so cold
and unfilled while just across the street

this new motel has human beings who can
spend and do not even pause once in
mid-swallowing of good Grand Marnier

cutting the insides of their throats like
smooth honey, as some just across the
street consider cutting the outside of

their throats with steel; not once
in this opulence does a guest shudder
thinking of poor men who cannot fill

those they love or themselves with any
good things and even consider let alone
do anything about it . . . There is a

toughness in the breezes. All around this place
is the quiet of hard struggle and to
walk here is not safe. . . . If they think

you might be some big money from the motel
you have asked a starving man for your life
and he'll take it for his life.

II

Here I was in a luxurious room with room service
and a balcony, but the maids in the hall when
I passed them saw penury in the set of my mouth fixed

forever in fatigue and endurance's look and
on their hands and knees scrubbing carpets
and the halls of the motel hallways, if they wanted

their jobs, one or two of these lovely ladies smiled
at me enjoying that one of them had somehow managed
to be a guest, and if I had wanted to imagine

that I could get away with being anyone but
who I am, a sweeper like them, their knowing
smiles as I passed them told me I fooled no one.

I was like an elderly trick passing Queens thinking
that growing old ever hides your soul, that
you're "everybody's make" . . . no it wasn't sly suggestion,

their smiles and looks knowing me, no, it wasn't that
their postures on their hands and knees forcing
their bottoms to elevate as if they'd do anything in

my mind for a twenty dollar bill, no there was no
offer, even if growing old I yearned for there
to be one more offer . . . just one more! Once more

heads turned cruising me—no matter my fantasy
wishes, there was nothing more in that hallway
than my dirty images and just one or two

worn out human beings knowing
another when they
saw one . . .

III

I was so common and familiar
in my conversations with desk clerks
that when the elevator was tied up

by maids moving their carts
from floor to floor, they had
no problem suggesting

I use the Service elevator which meant walking
through their kitchen passing garbage and through
their laundry room to ride with the Room Service

waiter who knocked on my room door with reverence, now
a knit brow disturbed frown as he really saw me now
next to him riding up in his shit, and though

he was young and couldn't put it together, he too
sensed I was more an older him than a guest here
yet he knew in seconds as the Service elevator

got me to my floor, he would have to resume
catering to me. I'll always wonder if he suddenly grew up
in that realization . . .

IV

The desk clerks knew only too well
I was in their motel on an ingenious low rate
plan . . . you dial 800 information and ask

for the package number . . . owing everyone but
life gets so pressed you blank your conscience
temporarily of the people you telephoned

in horror about the wage garnishee and phone turnoff
if they didn't rush you money . . . but if
you don't do this you won't live to pay them back, worse,

you won't be alive to be the person they sent cash.
Man has to escape out of his cages for
new breath . . . I. . . . just. . . . did it!

There isn't any excuse to do what you wish when you owe!
But I did it to survive and not use or drink
or have a coronary for principle.

Should this make me disreputable, dishonorable,
at least I can be told this personally
and not through the grass of my tomb. . . .

. . . and up in the hallways thickly carpeted like
bath towels the maids on their hands and knees were
washing carpets and the walls vulnerable

to my stare at their bottoms raised in air
strung out here along the hallway like so much
breathing meat bereft of their dignity as

they put out their flesh for food and roof. We motel guests
gorged and drank as if poverty were not
close death whispering dying along

the bedposts of luxury. Evil dressed its best.
Poverty had started to harden us beyond
the ability to ever enjoy again, but at

this motel that succeeds because the help's picked
from immigrants, I saw a chinese or vietnamese woman
maid all expression of joy erased from her naturally

stoic disposition, blank, only her mouth
without even her lips moving let words, like
hollow echoes from a pebbled well, out if

spoken to; she was desperate lest one
of her answers lose her this work. . . . This
small vietnamese or chinese woman she

seemed to appear out of the walls, probably a
service elevator as I would come and go in
and out of our room . . . pushing a heavy long

cart with everything on it to make rooms up
just about all this little tiny woman could push
by people like me there for comfort and pleasure

from our new depression given us for our faith and
vote by our President for being the fools we
always are always allowing the lie that it's

the Welfare Indigent not the wealthy who are
responsible for our loss of jobs, pensions
medical help . . . soon the years you can

still climb three flights of stairs on two sides
of twenty one buildings if you have to and
sweep one all the way down and climb up the next

or do anything but sit in the corner
of some Reagan club soup kitchen shelter
will be gone . . . of course

I'm to blame
but dying isn't easier because
you deserve it. . . .

To War Dead

Boys who walk through coffin blossoms
I do not know why you die
Leaving our young women like penguins with great open flippers
Because you have slipped forever out of their arms.

Leaves of you young flowers fall
Like shook horse-chestnut trees.
You drop at my feet like field mice
Caught in meadow fire.

Boys, your cries screech my dreams.
We advance to live on the moon,
Slaughtering our world behind us;
Leaving no trace that we were ever brothers.

The Treachery of Flame

Something has changed us, the wild grapes.
Excitement is in other imaginations of our taste,
to keep wish for us. Now we have been seen, fingered,
and picked over. We have squirted whatever we had,
the market is crowded, so to stand out one must
be impossibly rare. We have merely been the
new blossoms who come along, show and are gone.

Winter

Look at lakes, now shattered mirrors meld.
Water we have sunk in holds us up.
See! Evergreen over there! While some
hard wood, Maples, Elms, seem death bent but
as sure as thick white snow is frozen water webbed,
birds will be back in those trees replenished in green leaf.

The Shadow of a Leaf

I

We lie into disintegration underneath leaves
if we are not cremated and scattered
when our breath has gone back to the air.
It is as if we are in a never realized Portrait;
our breathing prevents the finished picture,
and without our breaths something isn't in it.

The fixtures, houses, meadows, fences, trees
thick and hazy, vast magnificent view
are there forever for the wonder of next humans
unless Nuclear removes them. In rage of our
inner instincts suggesting to us that the world
is a vacuum area we fill until we don't, revolt

at our recognition of this but helpless,
seems to become inner fury turned cowardly vengeance.
We kill because removing from among us seems
the worst we can do to anyone. Yet what do you call
what you do with no certain result!? Who can hurt
what is knocked out? We only know how much we cling

to this space we're in, how we don't want to leave
this unfinished ever changing earth, yet we
even kill children whose lack of life experience, perception;
seeing violence attracts death defying behavior that
seems exciting not ever believing they can die . . . only
old people die. . . . We have no wish to watch

and retch on smell burning stench or to see hanging.
The moment they kick you out whirling a rope,
sinking, he fell through himself with a snap.
His life burst shut off blood through the skin
of his face like a bruised purplish plum.
Needles with overdoses, life goes in a tremble

as soul tries to creep by interrupted heart rhythm
in silent cleanliness without odor, seemingly
unviolated human on a rolling cart as if asleep
but never to wake as we exhale our imagining

he's suffered by vanishing before we do.
We know he's lost his life but what a let-down

after we've taken it, we can never be sure what is sure!
If, indeed, eternal paradise is our reward for dying, then
why kill a man into eternal joy! The man now dead is unable
to conceive punishment. Since not one of us is or
ever has been dead, we cannot know if we really deprive him.
Fear become a thrill of sending someone there without

our going, the nearest we can come to this fear of ours.
We are watching ourselves die . . . and will we die for our
sins or Paradise . . . ? He is now seeing what I'm fearing to
   see.
He is now seeing what I'm denied to see, so, in this
moment of his death is envy . . . even in the act of vengeance
you escape me in your knowledge now and I wish

I could call you back for a moment, rip
tombstones to ask you, burst your coffin and give you
your life in exchange if I must to ask
you not did it hurt but what do you know now . . .
The blind dread what they cannot touch.
We who can see do not see at all.

      II

You invite me to lunch, I think you
mean me to present myself at your front door,
ring the bell or rap my knuckles and
you'll beckon me into a fine sitting room
where we will have refreshment and chatter
before my salivating expectation is led
to its satisfaction. But no, I come

to your front door, but you block
my entering, standing with a picnic basket slung
on your arm like a trunk of gluttony
and you're carrying a big blanket. "Come," you
tell me and we go out back of your house
to a rather rough rock clumpy green cow pasture.
There are even cows here and there.

"Sit," you instruct me. You throw out the
blanket like a charade to a non-existent on coming bull
and, as for all the lucky, it settles for you
well enough. "Sit," you say, "we'll eat! I've
got good cold wine and chicken. I wanted
you to have lunch with me on this old pasture
because a very famous battle was fought here.

"Look how flies still hover buzzing, not just
over cows and us but expecting.
How warm serene the green is here under the sun.
But once men butchered each other right here,
blood rushed the gasps of hope.
This picnic blanket grass
was bayonet death's green.

III

"Come now, let us go inside, serenity is freezing.
Yes, sit, look out the window in this room of the living.
Now sit, listen, hear! Ghost shadows will always
materialize and vanish where telephone wires carry
our living voices still, underneath the electric hum
is the chorus of all those who lie forever in earth and

"where they've gone the buttercup they've become
does not tell, nor can you and I but picnic here.
All the actual that took place is happened
without consulting us and we can only imagine
out of imageries, Television, our dreams of
remembrances we are not even aware we ever noticed."

We can only assume we know what took place
as we give to all told tales our individual
identity's response. All our answers lie
in search and if we ever get a glimmer
of why human carcasses were birthed to forever
fight stink and for cleanliness, it is, truly,

as if somehow very procreation was to live to grow
up for death, dying. The God we live by wants us
created, it seems, to die for His Eternal Paradise . . .
Why is it told that "He" came to us, here on

our earth to grotesquely die, as if we asked Him to, what
say did we have in what must be done so we could be

saved from an unseen unknown Forever! Just what
occurred in this place Eden that we don't get AIDS for today,
    and,
sacreligious, we are assured on television that we've
"been to Mass" if we just watch it on Channel R, a soft
soothing washer woman voice reassures us that we are
not to worry about losing our immortal souls

if we watch Mass, the TV show. After, we can, apparently,
be and do as we wish, blinding ourselves, blocking out that
Eternal Hell is supposed to await us if we grapple
with and give in to doing and thinking everything
and anything we like as lust, desire urges. . . . What on earth
will dear Christ have to do next time He comes

to win us Paradisiacal Forever, jump out of a plane aflame
as old time Rockers "The Grateful Dead" sing
"They Know Not What They Do" and land unhurt so
we'll believe it's really "Him," instead of
bringing Lazarus back, He Himself does such another trick
in our sophisticated age as to quickly win us back to

purity from scepticism but what is this!? Why must
"He" come to us again if "He's" already been here!
Why is "We must have faith!" screamed into us from
a first message in our umbilical cords if "He's"
been here! It's like telling children, don't
take a cookie I'll be watching when they know

in their confused little heads that you've left
the house. They've got Authority Figure, the
Keeper of Hair-brushes for their cherubic fat
bare bottoms if they answer back or ask
"how can you see me if I take a cookie if
you're not home?" . . . Oh, you who have gone, call back!

Whisper! Come to us in our most secret sleep.
Tell us what you know now. . . .
If this Christ died for my sins did Christa McAullife
die for propaganda too!? Last time "He" rose from

the dead, that was stunning, before Space Craft
which "He" allowed us as if being willing to beat

his best earthly feats if it will get us to believe
what we cannot know or call back about to those who doubt,
think death is dead and dust and that's it.
Why did "He" come? What was necessary to insist
on making us with brains, feelings, reason only
to vanish no one knows where, it seems

almost genius to be cremated like
dust thumbing itself at dust but in
an urn and forever possible to have the jar you're in
picked up by a living hand and waved to the world,
that always seemingly never complete picture because
you're not in it and never ever were but look alive

physically on earth always looking caught yourself, your
image caught in some camera photo but only the temporary
person within, existing on this earth and vanishing, to be
looked at a hundred years in future by eyes who know
human beings photograph differently several times in any
week or day of their supposed lives as if we are never meant

not ever really to be seen as we really looked by anyone . . .
   ever
as if we truly in God's scheme, we're never here but just
flesh on skeletons allowed for awhile
The Devil's hope, excitement, anticipation
as if these really exist, but the second we're
satisfied we forget yearning.

Here you are only the temporary person in meadows
and jammed shopping Malls you and those of the past
and of future, always keeping the great canvas called
the world like an unfinished picture, all the
totally finished work is in the basement of the
earth's museum, graves. Finally putrified, then

dust to materialize into you, supposedly
in God's Paradise . . . But do we!? No one who has gone
tells us. Sometimes at night if we walk out in
deep bitter cold a sense of something trying to touch us

chills us more and in warm climates too this feeling comes
in the low key humidity, that the wind, soothing or even

extreme silence is trying to touch us, get our attention
with a message, information . . . is it from you who are gone?
What did we do!? Execute the bad into where the good go,
where we're supposed to go when we vanish from where
we now sit looking out at such serenity of life and color
and wish in the emptiness. Cremated, at least the urn

we are in is forever possible to see again and pick up
off our small safe graveyard shelf above ground.
Here once was I and am now dust but visible forever, not
sinking in earth's stink skeletal and looking like
no one but everyone, yet as we leave this life
it is wished we would not hush but tell

what we know now. Life is quiet.
We make all the noise there is in the world.
Otherwise, without our noise
the earth is as quiet as earth. Here in this house now,
we can look at vacancy though it appears
rich fields and flowers and knowledge

of what has happened here can seem to make a permanence and
a continuance but if only those who have been
could tell us what they know.
As we leave this it is wished
we would not hush but
tell what we know now.

IV

These once ploughed fields left suddenly, as if
the Farmer was called out west where he went.
But Scotland, Connecticut grew wild trees, roots
over Herbert Smokler soil turned to grow not to
vanish in weeds like snakes in insane hair.
Here, a grave dug with no committees met to say

you couldn't stay in the very earth ground of your
whole life but must be put in a prescribed meadow
with everyone you never knew. Well, you never ever

spoke to them anyway, so your silence
will always be normal, usual, though
you are buried away from what made

sense in your living at all "forever." You
are gone forever. What do you know!? It must
be all right or everyone would not allow
nondescript removal. . . . Please at least call back!
you can't? . . . then . . . hint what you know, eery even
in what we think comes to us when a door slams.

Imagining is only concluding from an unknown noise
or sight or something put to us we think we
understand like the Carnival Barker's descriptions.
Life's circuses making us think we see a dangerous show,
thrilling to the sight, so give us a hint what
Eternal Paradise is or isn't. We're disappearing anyway!

Hint what you know. I know what you know! No
I don't but I think I do but thinking I do know
does not make it all right with me to leave, no. Could
flesh on us hold up two hundred years, a thousand, Forever!?
What would we have to take to preserve our carcasses
where we're used to being, right here, I want to

stay right here where I know fright and feeling
and can recognize that I enjoy at least the
idea of lust and it isn't dark. Noise is insinuation
and undoubtedly wrong concluding, but one can think,
one can see others, we can think we know
what's around the corner and where we've been!

V

Underneath leaves that pirouette before they
drift to become crisp on top of the ground
easily crushed into disappearance, they
fall smartly alive but finally crumble to vanish.
All the bright colors they were drawn from, the
unpainted picture, into brown crushed frozen

in cold autumn, the victims of cold as we lie
underneath the earth they are gone from too, if

we are not cremated or scattered to become
thoughts in heads of the living, often our features
almost materialize in human thinking as memory
recalls and puts our features to what is being remembered.

We are the unknown faces in dreams good and disturbing,
people remember having after awakening and wonder who
the person so urgently communicating with them in their dream
was, it was us trying to call back what we know because
in the vault of human filing of experiences, observations
glimpsed in a flash, forgotten, filed somewhere

in regions of human brain undefined yet, we ourselves beg,
ask those who disappear to whisper to us in our sleep or
create scene in a dream of how this emptiness we fill
with despair and only by hoping, gets better somewhere! Where!?
. . . just in the shadow of a leaf, the beauty
the world made itself into from Glaciers

and eruptions is the end of our being in it, the
canvas, perhaps, the great landscaping of James Ruddock, yet
new people contemplating, mostly oblivious or where would
involvement, personal drive commitment ever come from of
me acknowledged and that whatever we do is for another's
  memory.
We are gone and no one can know if we need help . . . because
  we don't

call back . . . and in all our discoveries we must achieve
a way to call from here . . . *Hell is here knowing that*
we are born, developed, informed, experienced
and come to like and desire but leaving what we know!

Eden's real curse on us from a God who says
we bear guilt.

The leaves vanish but are in the buds of Hardwood . . . it is
only we who are here once and vanish, replaced
by the muscle that took purity in a garden and
must forfeit whatever life it initiates, doomed
and will not be here long. We are driven
to create what cannot survive but leaves, oh, call back! Beethoven
  where are you?

Statues, bridges, cathedrals last forever but they
who envisioned them and then drew sketches, designed
and built them in the never completed canvas earth are gone
   . . . forever.
Unless God has changed his mind, Planet travel in light years takes
only one of our earth life but the world goes by one hundred
   years . . . perhaps,
like toll booths, enough has now been collected of us.

The Gunman and Other Poems

This Is a Stick-Up

El Welfare Chevito slunk out of his urine stench Casa
to feed a needle to the fella sitting down on the nerve ends
 of his bowels
like some impaled Prime Minister slipping his feet on a greasy
 pole
where he can get up off and can't.

Evening just turned dark touched lovely people like you and me
with soft caressing breezes, but El Welfare Chevito like a victim
 of croton oil.
Crave jabbed murder onto his relief-screeching brain. Pastrami-
 gorged police
sitting on the wide buttocks of no exercise, waited to get their
 sex with six guns.

And up the avenue innocent victim in the white apron of piety
that concealed the one-eighth worth of Virginia ham he gave you
 after
you paid him for half a pound, made the slot man at the Daily
 Spread Eagle
his morning headlines for the big shots laying cents down for a
 copy
like it was nothing.

It was over in a minute, light flashed on light
throwing the good guy's glasses off his sneak thief's surprised
 eyes
stamped with a gasp muffled by his shoulders hitting groceries
falling all over him like stir crazy cons leaping hopelessly
 nowhere.

But outside, slinking up with their winking whore's light
to kill forever the seed of a life, the wide blue bottoms
had El Welfare Chevito blasted into street with so many holes
 in him
it was hard to get in a last dream of faraway Puerto Rico.

On the Eve of My Becoming a Father

I have turned now in the night and
all my blown-away kisses of our familiar love
with the words and sillinesses
always thrust by nature's drive,
lost in the loneliness of our sighs
in the dark, in darkness even with
blazing lights on and booze
to slobber down our failure
so we could turn on our pillows
as if we did not know each other.
We had been every place but this
and our travel folders were worn out.
I had been about to hang up my gun
but the hammer shot one spark into the moon,
so magnificent, it is beyond me.

As an Apple Has Iron

Astronauts, jumping stars like stream pebbles
into the sun's blood yoke, we are all travelers
if risk is proven removed, but now you cannot
open your enclosed faces on, say, Venus of sweet
confidence, "the beautiful white one," "the
mistress of the heavens." I had hoped as Galileo,
that beneath Venus bed covers of clouds lay a virgin
Brazil, a new place to begin fresh like Australia
once, America, for the world grows weary, but all
oxygen of Venusian oceans lies locked in rusty
planet surface, the air we need to live immediately
taken by the iron to become rust as here on earth
an apple has iron and bitten into, exposed by our
teeth, opened to oxygen becomes rusty brown and dies.

What will we find of the Moon or Mars and the others,
astronauts who cannot step out of their get-ups to find
if anything smells like rich green new grass of an
earth spring rain. You are curiosities pitted
against the impossible.

Mundelein on the Michigan

Great blue and lake birds
skimming night off dawn
with the fingernail of a quarter moon
when I am alone with early morning
as it slips off its black gown.

Out of bed with the morning awake,
it is in this new hour of days
that I am my best and there is
Lake Michigan like a trapped big tear.

I came in on a plane fresh
from shadows and angles
where my moves are to survive, screaming the
condition of a bumblebee down an air shaft.

And my heart knows the anguish we must control.
I will go and be gone and your fresh beauty will be
for others, damned as I am to
cry for the wounds that break us.

Bird squadrons low over the water
yellow, gray, white, blue, according
to sun shades and wind spray, but
it is not my life, I am the
wolf with a lamb in his teeth,
why did God turn me around!

Of the Betrayed

I give you ashes.
No one can find
which dust is your son.

No young girl will ever lift
the blankets of darkness delighted
at his sword in her.

No young child will ever
pinch a nipple of his breasts.

No young girl will ever cry
he left her.

No young child will finally
stammer the word father
to his proud hearing.

No, we will not have these things
to concern ourselves of him
and I will never have him either
nor you, nor anyone. He
is the fertilizer of grass.

Yes, I remember him,
he came in with sideburns
to his jawbones. First
we took his wavy hair, then
innocence out of his eyes
and stamped death into the pupils.

We robbed him of his chance on
the earth, turned him on his
fellow man so that he undoubtedly
felt he had the explosion coming
that stained his knees with his life.

He hated us in heartbroken weeping
not knowing any more than you do
where he was going when
he closed his eyes and could not open them.

I give you his ashes
mingled with others.
See them, can't you see them!

Penobscot Poems

Lobster Claw

I

Morning and I
must kill.

Rise in one-bulb light, trying
to move quietly through
thin asbestos-braced house
shuddering at each of my steps,
the one-bulb light crashing
black dying night to
cowardly dawn, ashen at
our endeavor, so quiet
a twig snap jolts me,
as unwelcome surprise to all murderers.

Lobster, I will kill you now,
crouch in your rocks. Pull up
your bed covers of seaweed.
Ride the sea's bottom. Move
out deep in winter. Burrow
in mud. Hide under
kelp. I will bait you
to my family's survival
without conscience. My own
life is in the lines hauling you in.

The sea will rage to
upset my boat and have
you grabbing me in your
right crusher claw into
your efficient stomach
grinding up Mollusks, Algae,
and each other. But I
am a survived victim of
old storms. The ocean shrugs
at my approach.

I go, tired, braced
for you by determined

necessity, hope in me
that I can keep my
children from having to
laden their tables
by slaughter, fearing
I never can.

Lobster, let us
get this done. God
you must want me to
do this. Perhaps
the ocean with all its
bluff is not big enough
to keep all you lobster.

I will lay out a string of
redfish-baited traps you
cannot resist.

II

I am an old timer and
give my whole days.
Youngsters no longer
work the long hours, they
come in off the water early
and go to watch rooster-crowing
contests, fight and drink.

The sea is a womb, frothy
like blushing lovers are
shy, but within her,
after all, are the lives
of her many children
killing among themselves,
and she strikes down hard
those too naive to learn
that she is a sea not to be taken.

I am not easily caught,
but overwhelming fatigue
is my nemesis.

III

It is over, men like me
out in boats in the
great sea days. Airplanes
spot you now, lobster, scuba-divers
pluck you taking away your
choice to stay hidden
in ocean bosom or
try to outwit the trap and
win the bait.

We were a breed of men
who could keep such
generated strength in our
sinews and wills as to
break the back of a bear
on a handful of food a
day and walk a hundred
miles, only our
open wilderness is the sea
with hoop net pots
made from iron tires
before Parlor traps, Double
Headers, long gaffing from
small boats on our
bleached-out green rock
coast in blizzard winters,
endless fog summer days
dug into your bones and
never lets go a grip
that inner endurance must be
forged by us to survive,
until, as cow punchers
too long from women we
come in off our water
for fertility ritual and
blood.

IV

Saturday night is
always our time. On the
sea we think of
our women, but mixed
in is the blood of good fights.

Nothing drives a man so
half out of his head as
work that never is enough
for his women and
children, never able
to give your woman
pretty things, your
youngsters something
better than lobstering,
our wind-burned lives
turned old, desperate.

Looking at our thin
frame houses, our pinched
women and our sons
will be out on the
boats with us soon, our
girls rushed to
the first men who
will support them,
whether there is love.

So, the boats in, tied
to their docks, an
edge of ice on the
evening wind, traps
piled to dry on
the wharves, we
walk by tourists come
to Clem's Pound,
picking their dinners
alive out of the day's
haul, frantic in
tanked salt water.

Home, our women
know there is no
stopping us, not
pouring all the liquor
their Baptist hearts
detest will mull
us from this
relished night.

V

There is a dance over to
South Thomaston, Postmaster's
son there from New York wearing
the city clothes of a
man who looks like
he never worked and
Woberton Edgecomb
walked over ready
to break his face
like hitting a glass
lampshade quick,
pulling your hand
back so fast you
don't skin a knuckle,
but the face
goes apart like
it never existed.

But they were talking
instead of going
at it, not
throwing a blow, him,
Postmaster's son
speaking soft, unriled
and damned if
he didn't reach out
and shake Woberton's
hand talking about
how they were through
high school together,

asking Woberton how
he'd been.

That was it! Out on
the sea, the ocean
sure don't ask you or
Clem paying us
grudgingly for our
lobster, but
Postmaster's son
was a Maine boy and
knew us, our
self-contained resentment.

But this here was
our Saturday
night to break heads,
ravish women for our
helplessness, our lives
always on the sea floating
and just then Elmer Tippett
come into South Thomaston
dance hall from Saint George,
the foreigner from
Houlton who'd married
his sister with him. None
of us liked the idea of
his having the little
Tippett girl. Houlton's
Potato country and we're
Lobstermen.

I know the pine trees shook
in their roots when
Woberton Edgecomb turned
his punch meant for
Postmaster's son
and hit the Potato farmer
up off South Thomaston
dance floor like a
barn door struck by
a tractor.

But Potato fellas
can hit too, that's
the fun of it!

The getting the sea
and futility out
of you Saturday night
while your women wait
in thin frame houses
wondering how much
of you will have
to be put back together.

That Potato fella
was up at Woberton
and they were
spraying each other's
blood for their years.

I looked to take on
Postmaster's son
come visiting our hell,
then to go back
to his soft city life, the tourists
at Clem's Pound taking their
time selecting our
days' haul like cannibals
over their ruined prisoners,
turned me to murderous
hatred and right then
Postmaster's son would
have gone home in a
basket of my aggravation, even
if he did ask Woberton
how he was, but
Postmaster's son
was gone, using
the kind of brains
that escaped him from
the boats everyday life,
come home one time finally
busted apart, either

by a Saturday night
fight, Southern Comfort
full up back seat
auto fornication, or
the sea at last
too much to take on.

VI

Lobster, colored
blue green, sky blue,
bright red, and even
albino, I'll find you.

I string my baited traps
each dawn and come after
them in the afternoon, and
the later I come back the
more of you lobster are
in them.

If you're "shorts," too small,
I throw you back, cursing
my waiting, my labor
for a lobster like you,
not big enough to bring
in and sell.

In the whole seas of
the world, Rockland, Maine,
is your home, lobster,
vulnerable shedding
your shell, helpless
as larvae floating
the ocean and later,
weak of your many
joints, claws, your
body easily snapped.

No one ever forgets the
sweet taste of lobster
claw meat driftwood

fire cooked beneath
steaming heaps of seaweed.

I must go out through
thick early morning
fog until sun burns
it off and I can
see. It is in this
darkness and then the
black of evening, when
I wearily ache, that I
could go wrong. So,
Morning I watch you,
and Evening, my eyes
are on you from noon.

Something I
did not consider, flame
near the boat's gas tank
could take me, and
it was the last thing
on my mind when
the blast threw me a
half mile all cut up
in pieces for you, lobster.

VII

I'd rather finish
spitting at sea spray
that has slapped my
face fifty years,
than in some chair, but
my woman has spent
our lives waiting for
sundown when I
come into her arms.
Ocean, I owe her
some time and
Lobster you shall
not deny her.

No, Lobster, you shall
not have me. My
woman would like
to see once again
what I look like in
daylight for awhile
before we are no more
than the faces of clouds.

And all the heavy rain
down on lobsterman already
fighting the water that
is ocean, is our tears
weeping for knowledge
of him.

It is the sea mother
who whips him in a
wrath of wind like a
snarling cornered cat
while lobstermen
rip out her children.

So, to it then and
a day on the sea, fresh
wind and salt free
feeling. Tossing
the bowed trap, whichever
you think takes
strain best and I
take my chances on borers,
rather than risk
termite-treating
the traps and lose the
haul.

Morning again, and I must kill
to exist. Lobster,
scavenger crustacean,
why should I so mind
killing you!

Tell Her That I Fell

Woke me retching and alone.
Within doom booze
her arms around me again
in wished-for honeymoon time
that never happened.

Wait now to become ashes
and am so sorry.

Stagger now, shaking for what I'm running on.
But it takes a few to get started these days,
face gouged by razor unable fingers hold
and each step away from where a bar is near
makes me feel certain I'm going to drop dead.

Each morning now is terror.
The bathroom mirror reflects
earthworms have not a long wait
to pick me clean.
My toothpaste mouthwash
is a breakfast of liquor,
so is all day and every complete night.

Took her once in the snow
the seacoast near, vivid
like if bright red blood was blue.

Afterward when she stood up
the bare spot we melted
was like two halves of a pear.

I know she is in a Fishing Village now
with many babies.
The boats go out each morning before sunup
breaks through salt fog and come in long after dark,
just to make ends meet.

Maybe he is good to her
in his clumsy understanding
I hope so, but never sure in his mind.
Furiously suspicious at any man's glance at her,

eternally looking for whoever I am
directly into the face of each tourist who comes
into town.

How it frustrates him, unable
to find and strangle me
who is always the wedge between his best effort,
and he is so strong, sea life hardened.

Wake me these days retching then, all right
just tell her that I fell.
My happiness time was with her,
been any kind of a man
I would have carried her like
a knapsack away and felt
her feet slapping my thighs.

Come on, death, I fear
to wobble the few steps to you.

Dark Horses Rushing

Mathew Brady
    there's an old shack now
              by the stones
with auto tires hung on nails
    below 7-UP signs and from inside
the nasal adenoid indigestion-giving
              holla of Bob Dylan.

But I swear, Mat, just as I pulled
    into the Filling Station,
              Dylan shut off a minute,
and I could hear horses riding hard
    like death in pursuit of itself.

Ages now, Mathew Brady,
    have accomplished Infrared camera
we can point at a group of rocks
    insignificant now alongside
super eight-lane highway
    driving up through the breasts
of Georgia to the moon in her crown.

Near Infrared, closer catching image
              left by body's heat
will show up a ghost to my great-granddaughter
              where a corn-haired Confed boy sat
on those stones asleep in the dream of his lady
              and the blue-coat boy shot him dead
standing up like a despicable Fox hunter
kicked out of the lair for a week
              in birth of baby fox time,
big wide grin on his face wiped out
              by a good three-hundred-yard shot
that took measuring the wind by the eye
              of Confed buddy over yonder
and gunsmoke choked the tears out of leaves.
Then dark horses rushing
    inside thunder
as both sides scattered
    for the life God gives us once.

Watching Jim Shoulders

When did my manhood wake to its dying!
Never in New England or in Elko, Nevada, inside
screen doors with legal girls, dulled by fifty-cent splits.
But in Colorado's air and snow like first communion lace on
blunt mountains. He was Mantle on horseback, the
same class, and as injured, out of that remote private
America of ranges, ranches, vast wide-open space where
sophistication is silence. Truth is your action shot
from corrals, lasso wrist flicked instantly with
eight seconds to rope and tie or lose. Shoulders,
scraping the cheeks of steers along earth cut by
grooves of his boot heels, while those horns that could
cave in ribs, turned until the folds in the animal's
neck looked like its spine would split through skin,
yet didn't in this master's hands.

Shadows

I cannot look at birds or hear
them singing. We failed
to be men in the flood of our youth,
how can we ever be old men!
We will be shadows, shells
of carcasses rocking on porches
until the wind explodes us
and we are the foul smell
in the air turning the noses
of lovers and children, in
some vague future peace time.
I have nodded to God and
He looked right through me.

Closed Wake

Silence, I am seeking quiet.
My insides no longer burst to flowers
or hay like the smell of sun
on the back of your hand.

My foot smacked rivers,
and I paddled canoes on pure water,
before defecating boats, until
animals would not come to drink.

We packed our bags for a planet,
leaving only tombstones.

After exhausting calcareous tissue
of all the slaughter, we dug Indians up,
shipping their bones to make buttons.
Now computers stalk us.

I love the woods. All the
wilderness is come down.
We are in cages of mortar.
Our open plains become skid rows
of the flood tide of penises
until cactus needles wilt.
If we had only used our brains instead.

A Hen Crossing a Road

Frenzied Sunday dinner
sensing the way we size her up
with the sensuous look of anticipating pigs
waiting to wallow our faces in her flesh.
Bobs, weaves, back and forth
from the yard gravel too near the chopping block;
darts no straight path across
the old dusty dirt pebbled road and comes back
noncommittal, flapping courageous wings.
When the Ax falls
refuses to be dead until she has run her blood out.

Old Gravestones

See them in morning mist like fingernails of
some gigantic hand ripped up
through the hard ground trying with some unseen
massive shoulder ripple thrown through dirt to
get them all back on earth to live. Death was so
quick. In the old cemetery chipped slate bent like
loose teeth in this head of earth. The short years
on the stones. Infants hardly out of the womb, dead.
Now the world moves too fast. Man is down to his
last breath and his youngsters, with graveyards
staring at them, stalk tombstones, enraged,
wandering in among our sanctified history that we
treasure in our fear of oblivion. Carved angels
with halos and wings, legends chiseled into stone
that prove we are immortal here on earth forever, but
in rage, in raging anger our young kick them down,
desecrate, destroy the preserved memory of vanished
men, in rage against quick dismissal by us into
earth forever with an old gravestone all that's
left of them.

Old Orchard Beach Maine Burned Down

Fire has leveled my baby's toyland.
We are father and child in the same place.
It was my playpen too, Sea Weed beach
and the sense of salt and sand on
you and sunburn.

Town of Merry-Go-Round and Donkey cart
rides in dark underground tunnels through
the wonders of horror, down a simulated
mine shaft full of ogres that leaped out
at you. Ferris Wheels town of fun. Children
town burned down. Town of glee-filled laughing
youngsters and hideout motels for lovers right
over the beach. Town of people growing old
on their last time around.

Town for me once when I was young, and
I yearn to go back there now. Town a hurricane
ripped apart in my youth, throwing the Merry-Go-
Round I knew in my boyhood like a scaled saucer,
gone, as we took our only child back where I was
once happy, to a Merry-Go-Round in flames when
Old Orchard Beach Maine burned down, from a
heater too near dry wood and the wind was right.
Again all gone but the scent of fresh pine on
the sea's wind.

                                      turned back pages in an ancient
black and molded photo album, yellowing snapshots of
a chubby dark-curled boy and an equally chubby
light-curled boy in what were pinafore suits seated
on the sunny sand beside two huge-hatted choker-
dressed women . . . Aunt Annie and Mamma with the
spindly O O Pier poles and Casino in back, around 1916,
Jim Moore of Glen Cove, Maine, remembers and writes this poet,
. . . in another photo, dad, shirt sleeves rolled up onto
elastics and pant legs rolled to the knees, barefooted with
us boys . . and in a brown-covered, less molded book, some
earlier Jim Moore girl friends who got waitress and

Chamber jobs at some of the inns, with the same pier in back,
while still later, yes, a couple more blondy beaned boys looking
at the wonders of the old steam peanut machine engine and
cart at the inboard end of the Pier . . . Moore's own kids . . .

What child imagines his own child!
I remember walking these streets, a
boy with no idea that flesh I helped make
would one day love this place too and
be visible in front of my eyes on my memory
back when once I ran ragged swam this sea by
Googins rocks until bleary-eyed exhausted in
happiness, I could no more, but only sleep.

                            dancing out on the pier that fell down.
the old pier with its underpinnings
crammed into sand for fifty years
holding up the ballroom where the
big bands played out over the ocean.

                    There was a luncheonette on the
                    corner of East Grand Avenue that
                    served big thick mayonnaise pickle
                    crab-meat sandwiches squirting out
                    the side of the bread.

                    And perfect rainy movie days,
                    a swim in the warm sea with rain
                    falling on you and dry feeling smooth
                    as a pearl from the ocean swim, into
                    see Brian Donlevy playing "Heliotrope
                        Harry."

Gone, it's all gone, the town's still there, there
is a beach and ocean still, but it belongs to someone
else, the French Canadians, starving for a sea,
Old Orchard Beach Maine is gone for my
daughter too, at six she looked at me, at
only six and said out of her mouth
—"It will never be the same," yes, a six-
year-old said that, she meant they rebuilt
but not the fun games she loved, and she
knew it at only age six, they're gone, all

but the ocean, it's all changed but the
never-ending sea-pounding ocean in Old
Orchard Beach Maine, like a woman you loved
once and can't give up because she's old
and ruined, run down and lived in, but
it will never be the same with her any more,
however you look at her and love comes
back to you . . . love for her, you loved
her once, you couldn't catch your breath for her.

Out Jim Moore's Window

Out Jim Moore's window,
in the living room of his house in Glen Cove, Maine,
stealing this visit like a dart on a boomerang,
my blue Atlantic boyhood scrutinizes me off
the slip borders of the Penobscot across Strawberry Hill.

See through glass, over Jim's patio back lawn,
tough fading green that light went out of from salt,
the beautiful water of the cove unchanged.

I remember the boy who looked out on that sea water
knowing it would take him to the world,
to blind all this in his accomplishment.

All come back to me here
in the silence of maturity's afternoon.
Things go wrong. We fail.

I am no longer bursting juice skinny youth,
but a man staggered by risks. Yet back across Kittery bridge,
things to do still must be
and I can't come home until they're done.

The Clear Blue Lobster-Water Country

This trilogy is for
 Ida Elizabeth Carey Connellan,
  who was my mother

Book I
Coming to Cummington to Take Kelly

I

Father, we'll
meet again.

You can tell me you love me then.

I went to your Rice Paddy when
you gave me choice between prison,
running, or places I
had no right being, but
I love you, Father, love you.
It's a hot love. I wish
you loved me too.

You'd send me anyplace!
I need your love enough to go.
I stand unemployed now bewildered.
People look at me like
I'm something awful!

I'll show them! Father, help
me, I seek you, the
original dream.

I'll fight for your love!
Look what I do
for you.

Come to Cummington
to take Kelly.

Not Wilbur he's
True and Great . . . nor Herman Melville either . . .

. . . take a good look
at Port Hill Road, yes, it's
likely Kelly runs it, better face
facts, when you're taking a man on
you can get killed. He didn't

come for you,
you came for him . . .

Washington Irving, hold your
myth in that painting congealed.
Do not let them out again, that
crew, not yet, no
not for a while yet . . .

For you, Father, I
imagined up a contest.
Sought out an adversary
where none exists,
to win your heart beyond
the grave where I
never had it here.

We'll meet again and you
can tell me you love me then.

. . . Will my only child, daughter,
seek me out as I see you out!?

II

It is the nature of predatory
stalkers, failing to corner pleasure,
to slide into catastrophe, now,
of sexual monogamy, except
when she wants to have a fling;
and, thinking she failed me,
as I am come to feel I failed
you, Father, seek me out as I
seek you.

She is me in reverse, Father,
Young woman stalks the male now, she's
got the box to put it in and can
give a coronary of ego.

But she knows that my love
was hers . . . is hers . . . Father,
here I am as now age crowds
my youth out of sight . . . No one

in the world will see me
young anymore . . . only
my dreams are young.
And my lust is young.

Father, my child never has to wonder
if I love her, here it is
even written for her to see
when like the dry brown leaf
I am crumbled and gone.

My love is my wife's too, but she
was abandoned in your demand of me
and is full of disgust, annoyance
at the very mention of you. It is
my need to seek you, Father, she
is revolted by what you are, what
we, you and I were together
in Rice Paddies, as we were too
long ago in the trade of flesh.
. . . signing our Declaration of
Independence, calling ourselves
"land of the free" at
auctions of human beings.

For you, Father, I
come to Cummington
to take Kelly.

You did not know me
on this earth, Father,
resented to know me,

guilt full, guilt driven.
Violated, the child's
mother died when he
was seven and told she'd
gone to take care of a
little boy who needed
her more than he did . . .

Father, this while
you hung away from home

sniffing your lost opportunities
on the bum.

III

We come to Cummington
to take Kelly.

Should we really go
to Wellesley . . . ?

Is this "Kelly"
the "Kelly" we want . . . see
how it goes, Father, in my
invention . . . Coming To Cummington
To Take Kelly, a short folk song,
no, a cantilena by
El Bardo The Legend, your son.
Father, it will be easy enough
to concoct . . . Let's "Play Something!"
"Make Believe" . . . remember?
You sent us boys to Summer Camp
where my brother was
at home as moths in linen, but
I was despondent and lonely.

It was no place for me.
You did not know that
and meant only generosity
sending me too where
you sent the son you loved.

And in a crowd of bunk
rope cutters, Canoe
Paddle thieves I had to
keep my mouth shut and
not tell on them although
no one took me in their group
for keeping my mouth shut.

And punishment wasn't
a Counselor's touching you,
no, the grown men were too smart.

You don't whack paying customers
unless you catch them picking pockets
or something, you get a boy
to discipline boys. His name
was Kelly. It was horror.

I was wheat cut down by a scythe
I never did anything to, hit
and splattered fat lip, Father,
I can imagine him up for us, I will!

Wilbur, forgive my borrowing
Cummington.

Poverty allows few arenas.
My time is running out.

Still, my own imagination
must run its risk! Yet, it
would be treachery to tread
on Providence, Rhode Island,
Poe footprints, or
accost Emily Dickinson, to
combat someone in front of
her atrocity! . . . to try
to rescue Anthony Hecht's King
headed for flaying
would necessitate
going back into a
time I know nothing about,
better to fail trying
something I comprehend or
to win because I do.

"The strange man of the
mountain, his clothing of Dutch
fashion," has come for me.

"Figures in an old
Flemish painting that hung
in the parlor of Dominie
Van Shaick" come
for me now.

IV

Father, here is my scheme!
In "Running" by Wilbur,
Poem II 'PATRIOT'S DAY
       (Wellesley, Massachusetts),'
last stanza, page 27, in
"Walking to Sleep," lines 13 to 16,
clearly, Poet has taken his
little son to see little children run
of whom he says that one,
(which one!?) is . . . "our"
Kelley as big people have
Boston Marathon John Kelley . . . then
why stretch logic
even for you, Father,
to pick a fight go like
a sorehead bulbous nose
out of joint malcontent
to make trouble in serenity!?
Because the draw rope
on my well
is broken.

And with your horse
shot from under you
death coming from
all sides now, briefly,
fleetingly, you recall
with great welling of
anguish the places you
wanted to get to in
order to fix the rope
and bring up your dream again.

But standing in
dusty alone you die
as best you can absolutely
no good at it, with style
and a flair if this is
your last song you try then
to change your character

to be what the appalling
situation seems to require
that after a lifetime
against taking life you now
try to kill them well
so those who are left
will ride off, they won't
mutilate you, but will
look with honor on you
dead in the middle of their dead
. . . hoping a minstrel will come by
and see the great tapestry
of you and them and go
sing down the roads
of "El Bardo The Legend," "Lahty" . . .
. . . See what I mean, Father?
What silliness can be
thought up to capture
your heart.

But I have a simple plan
to run and box a man
to win your love
beyond the grave.

We'll meet again.
You can tell me you love me then.

One thing too, Father, there
will be no Roncesvals Gaston treachery
in this cantilena . . . nothing like
what happened to Roland! . . . It will be clean.
Truly dedicated too, to you, Father,
for you, Father, but dedicated to
Gauffridi of Aix and Giordano Bruno
burned at the stake, God forgive us!
For you, Father, dedicated to them.

V

Now, Father . . . . of all the
Kellys in the world why

go way up into the Berkshires
after one!?

Because it is high up there
and you have to go there
out of your way. I want you to
see me, Father, going out of
my way to do battle and
let's see what happens!

Father we'll "Play Something!"
Remember? . . . When I was a
little boy I'd walk along
talking to myself "Playing Something."
I'd come out of a movie slouched
with a cigarette hanging
from my Alan Ladd lip. I was
Graham Greene's James Raven
with the deformed wrist.

Now, Father, you and I will
do it again . . .

Look what I do for you!

This fat little gray man
with the potbelly snout
is Lahty!

Remember your "Lahty" singing
"Home on the Range" at age five
strumming on a cigar box banjo, remember
your "Boppledock!?"

Daddy do you remember your "Boppledock!"
. . . There wherever you are . . .

You just fell down
in front of a garage, the
cold stained concrete
grease like black blood
was your bed when you
hit that great bald head to death.

You were gone
and I didn't
have you anymore.

There wherever you are do
you ever think of Boppledock
with fat squirrel pouches Apple cheeks?

When they found you dead
the photograph of me
in your wallet was a
seven-year-old-boy photograph.

The photograph of my brother
was of him as a grown man.

VI

My brother and I never
had a chance to
like each other the
way we grew up was
each one for himself.

Full of hurt, heartbreak,
you screaming, "I
must be appeased!"

You screaming, Daddy!
Why, you were so
frustrated you used to
chew handkerchiefs
red in the face.

You'd pull a handkerchief
out of your pocket just
as you were about to scream
and bite down on it hard
like a man having his arm
cut off without anesthesia.

I think I know now
you were hustled
out of your dreams

before you ever
had them.

Your life was
disappointed in guilt
from birth to hesitate, to
scream at everyone like
anyone suddenly grabbed
and held and branded
not only white-hot on flesh
but deep within.

You screamed not ever
realizing why you
cried out which was
because yourself was
stolen from yourself
by Irish church and your
own ruined branded parents
bringing you up blessing yourself
in an age when to dare realize it
was beyond society's cope. So you
lived a wasted man, ruined
potential, you laid
on us, my brother
Young Billy and me as
it had been driven
into you like the
spikes in Christ's palms.

Your genius snuffed out,
I write it for you, Father,
because you are dead
and cannot ever now
have it all dawn on you
and write it for yourself, it
is a statement I make for you
because you can no longer.
A job I finish for you
only because I lived
long enough to and
love you.

We'll meet again.
You can tell me you love me then.

My love for you
overcomes memory, my
love of you, Father,
blots out the
horror of your screams
on the heart and joy
of my childhood your
screams like snakes of needles
aimed at inside my head
to somehow burn out
my reason, to smother
natural intuition,
comprehension . . . the
job got almost done
as it did with you.
But it wasn't accomplished
and this is my song to us
song of El Bardo The Legend
to his Father, to the world.

. . . In America, Washington Irving,
you have to be a peddler
of your wares, you can be
the great poet but only known
for smoking Pot, as something
funny running up and down
college corridors chasing
a boy not for poems!
We play to causes and audiences,
make sure we make everyone
feel superior, we're less
than they are, they don't
come up to us, we come down
to them or miss success is
where art is in America, Washington
Irving . . . where is your
fantasy gone, your spell
woven for us along

the Tappan Zee, up
in the woods of the Hudson?

. . . Father, we've got to
get this out of the way, was it
a mistake you made I
constantly reminded you of,
something you lost
I reminded you of . . .

> . . . It was always whispered
> you were engaged to marry
> Mother's sister who
> took you her catch up to the
> annual family Christmas sing-
> around-the-piano where the
> family stentorian loud phonies
> burst forth in song as
> though something had been
> waiting all year to hear them
> and you "saw" Mother and
> that was "it!" No one ever
> explained how you dropped
> Aunt Cynthia. I knew her a
> long time, into my middle age,
> she looked relieved to
> have me her nephew, pronounced "Neview."

> . . . Did you, Smilin' Billy, sin!?
> Naw, not you! C'mon! If
> you did I like you, if you did
> you put me in good company.

You wouldn't take Mother away
from singin' round piano
would you . . . not you!

Was it hard
to take bringing me up?

No? Tell me no, then,
when we meet
tell me.

What soap opera! The show
apparently is "El Bardo The Legend And Fa"
or "Lahty And Father" on
two every afternoon
with my tears lost in TV sets.

Who can find the true American broken heart
in the Diarrhea Commercial.

    My only brother and I
    never had a chance
    to ever like each other.

    There is cruelty between us.
    Young Billy's self-protective
    defense is criticism.

    My brother Billy is
    full of advice. It's
    the dirty cracks that
    are hard to forgive.
    All the lousy remarks
    he felt there'd never be
    a way in the world he'd
    regret saying anything
    he felt like.

    He felt violated, afraid
    I'd sponge off him,
    rob him. He was robbed
    of his only mother too
    at only six and screamed at
    by his idol Smilin' Billy
    all his childhood forced
    to feel filthy, guilty
    about erections, girls,
    getting horny, rushed
    to Confessional in the
    church that was always
    changed after burdening
    mankind with dictates, as
    it suits itself, daring to
    tell us we'll never "see God's

face!" Father preaches down at
the Methodist church now and
over at the Synagogue . . . so,
God, I'll see you sometime. I
"see" you right now that you
forgive me because I am sorry,
because I want to come to you.
. . . My only brother had to run
for himself, to save himself, rush
for his own life from horror.
Thank God he did it.

Father, I have to say it,
this is between us, you
and old Boppledock . . . my
brother and I never
had a chance to be close.

We were robbed of
our mother and
cheated of each other.

We are the children
of violation.

"I must be appeased!"
You'd scream, Big Billy!
You'd stop your Chevy
right in the middle
of Main Street, didn't
matter, traffic would
be backed up, little
boys' nervous systems
never mattered.
"I must be appeased!"

You could be drooling
and see some middle-aged
baseball bat swinger
come along who once
hit one over the fence
and how you could
turn it off, the screaming

at us boys and turn on
charm becoming "Smilin' Billy"
discussing next night's
game and plays and the
second he left, an
hour later, an
hour later!, turn red
face screaming
"I must be appeased!" back on.

As grown men my
brother and I hardly
see each other . . . Father,
look what I do now,
imagine this whole
short folk song, work
it all out with a villain
I must go conquer like
one of your basketball
contests of nonexistent enemies
shooting balls through holes of string
to raving cheers forgotten
as soon as there was a new tournament.

VII

We come to Cummington
to take Kelly.

I who ran against
Buck Shot and won.

Is this "Kelley"
the "Kelly" we want?

See, Father, got to
work it out think of
everything . . . like
. . . After searching phone book years
and, physically, always Irish,
many Kellys, never "the" Kelly.
In "Running" by Wilbur, line
"who would win again"

drew our eyes to who
would win again, "Kelley,"
triggered odd hostile
resentment in us,
all fixes lived through . . . see,
Father, how this develops!
. . . The stanza could sound
like races prearranged
so all others are going
through running motions
surrounding Kelley, who,
in among them will win
again, rather than
what it was, a
cocky, confident champion
sure in himself he
would take anyone running
with him that day, his
danger would be not to
really run and so be
upset by Joe the
Garbage Man's son . . . is this
what we have here . . . Father!?
Really!? . . . Isn't Wilbur's
poem simply and only about
little children . . . How far
do I go for you, Dad!?

. . . The danger, Father, is
attributing ability to
children, in other words, insanity.
Exercising paranoia . . . see how far
I'll go for your love . . . went to
Rice Paddies . . . we'll
meet again beyond the grave,
you can tell me you love me then.

VIII

We come to Cummington
to take Kelly.

I who ran against
Buck Shot and won.

Could "Kelly" be
in Cummington?

Or is my Kelly boyhood
Summer Camp Counselor
bully of frightened youth
really now some Kelly of
South Boston's Breed's Hill,
beery faced with blank
little wormy eyes with
murdering busing blacks in them?
Embarrassingly, we
aren't having any
luck finding the Kelly
we want, a Kelly who
has vanished among Kellys . . . or
now we're grown up and, as
his victim, he's important
to us but he always eluded us
by never hiding because he
doesn't think he did
anything to hide from,
so in this irony
he is vanished.

I am looking for
a "Kelly" and believe
he's put an *e*
after the last *l* in
the name "Kelly" before
the *y* and is in
Cummington . . .

He was solid, stalky, freckled,
conceited and had never been hurt so
he enjoyed hitting.

Frightening thing was
that he really was good and
beat opponents his own

age and weight with blood
lust of joy in it.

Summer Camp Counselors
were afraid of him too and
fed him small boys to
hit, they'd make you
get in a boxing ring with
this Kelly and he'd expose
the coward out of you from
where you had fairly
well hid it. One day
you read Wilbur's
"Running," in Poem II
a "Kelley" was in it
"content" within this
run . . . Sure he would
win again, as he
had always won . . . your cracking
skull seized on what you wanted
to be true, too full of
vengeance lust to think
clearly, that Wilbur
was "noting" that a "Kelley"
was content within this
run, not him, he, "Kelley"
wasn't saying he was content
within this run or that he
would win again, no, he said
none of this, but your
temple-pounding desire to
find him obliterated
your even observing the
double intention underneath
reference to the Kelleys
of Boston Marathon, wiped
out your ability to
even see the name of
this runner . . . "Kelley"
not "Kelly" . . . worse, your
insanity prevented your

realizing there is no one
in the "Running" poem by
Wilbur really named "Kelley"
or "Kelly" . . .

. . . See, Father, my
thoughts have become
like caramel syrup as I
"Make-believe try" to make
this work for you . . . but
all things are created out
of an adolescence, maturity
risks fearing to chance . . . I
would rather fail at this, Father,
and try, than grow old scared.

IX

We're in Cummington to
take Mr. Kelly . . . Kelley?
So well hidden in the
Berkshires where no one
ever knows where
anyone lives if you ask them.

But I come to Cummington
to take him. Come to me Kelly
or I'll come to you.

You run, they say, but
do you box!? The Kelly
I want, I come to
Cummington to take, boxed.

We can pitch a tent
while we run a couple of
days to know the roads
a little, although isn't
running running? Keep
your shoelaces tied
and don't trip.

We can stay in a tent in
Cummington or in a motel

down below Deerfield on
Old College Road if
Whale Inn's full.

It's easy to track
if you know a place but if
you've just plunged in
few will help you.

The Chief of the
Fire Department in
Cummington wouldn't
tell you where someone
lived, but anyone
will tell you where
a road is if you give
its name.

> . . . One day in Summer
> Camp in your violated
> indignation . . . how
> do you explain violation
> and to whom? . . . pain
> horror screams screaming
> into silence.
> Like indignant unbroken
> child slapping back, you tried
> to beat up your own brother
> in that Kelly ring, Saturday
> night challenges to get in
> good with Counselors, ingratiate
> the camp . . . and you fixed it
> so your brother couldn't
> get out of getting into
> the ring with you, the beating
> fear of Kelly did that to you,
> twice as big and two years older
> than your brother . . .
>
> You went for your little brother
> who went for both your
> thumbs in the gloves like
> swollen noses, spraining

them both and then didn't
finish you.

No one ever took Kelly
who came from somewhere
around "Bawston" . . . is
Cummington where that
bastard Kelly is with a
fancy letter *e* faking
you out between the last *l*
and the letter *y*? . . . was
the Kelly you're after
a runner!? He was
a boxer . . . but was
he a runner!?

We've got to show him
we lived, survived,
grew up and have
lasted to run him down.

We're as big
as he is now.

X

We drive into Cummington
someone left out, child
whose father loved
his brother more than
he loved him, pulp of
flesh with goopy eyes in
an incubator, he hated you
for that and your mother
almost left him over it.

Now in your old youth
you still feel ache pang emptiness,
dry heaves of tears that
never come, they were
cried long ago. You
fantasize home again,
now the house jumps back

into your head, the
porch you crouched on
playing Cowboys and Indians;
the hallway from the
living room chair you
sat crouched in looking
at tree branches through
the side panel glass of
the front door slowly
waving, the wind in
them sound was like
your mother's dress
sounded to your little
ears in the middle of
mischief times you
heard her coming
down from upstairs, you
sat listening watching
those trees waiting for
your mother. She died
but they didn't tell you
that. They told you she'd
gone away to take care
of a little boy who needed
her more than you did and
you sat waiting for her to
finally finish with that
other boy and come back. Now
you see your father tossing
you out of the house onto
the porch when divvy
time came.

Now you drive 5–9 into
what imagination runs
crazy, yearning, fear
one is outside what
one's heart needs, one
is deprived so into the
serene luxury to be
taken in and embraced

at last by your father . . . you'll
find this Kelly and you'll
run and box him good to defeat . . .
And your father, Smilin' Billy,
will toss and catch apples
back and forth with you the
way he did with your brother,
wear a baseball cap cockeyed
visor turned to the side of his
head with you, the way he did
with your brother . . .
But the old man
is dead Rip Van Boobie!
Buried now under the tulips
of deciduous forever . . .

XI

Yet in a nursing home you
gave up a couple of skid row
wine blasts to get him in
away from those awful ones
with squirrels running intimately
up the arm of Smilin' Billy now
he's got strokes, you sat with him
alone by his bed in the dark
hospital room and put your
hand in his hand and
he knew you were there, he
squeezed it and the
broken doll's moonbeam
face, silly in blood clot,
smiled as he squeezed
your hand getting strength
from it as if you were the bouncing
rubber ball he was depending on.
And when nurse came in
he said from beyond his
stabbed apathy . . .
"You see, I have two sons!"

XII

We come to Cummington
to take Kelly.

Take a good look at Port Hill
Road, yes, it's likely Kelly
runs it, his legs in the
thighs of the machine of
himself, two hard rubber balls
squeezing pistons, not
sponges, his wind exceptional for
his age, only the fact of years
inhibits him and don't count on
that, yes, he does run up Port Hill
Road to maple-shaped red house
on top left across just down from
Gates' white house, the road
levels there.

Kelly trains running
Fairground Road running
right, a rough run, the
workout road Kelly runs
on, up Dodwells Road past
red barn weeping willows up
into night black green, up!
The Martini heart
now knows quitting time.

Perhaps . . . is Kelly
Kelly poor boy running
to Master whims, perhaps
that's it! He's bullyboy to
get summers in camp for
himself, Patriot Day running
champion to be favorite and
so sponsored . . . "get Kelly (Kelley)
he'll run for you!" . . . like
animals who run Triple Derbies,
then are put out to procreate
stagger among the daisies

until they break something
and are shot.

We've got to race him,
to finally make it with Father
in hallucination it's all for
children his fists broke.

XIII

We'll park by the Fairgrounds,
come up every day dressed to
jog, not saying anything, just
doing it, just get out of the
car and run the roads to see
if we can make them
and we'll be in everybody's
eye, probably somebody's
relative or forgotten
son gone a long time, home
from somewhere, recalled
on the rim of minds as a
ten-year-old, if dwelt on,
we, someone who never
existed here, but mistaken
for someone who did because
people do not wish to think
a stranger could just drive
into Cummington, get out
of a car dressed like their
neighbor runner and run up
and down through their privacy,
mistaken for someone they
all know, if they just stop
and think on it.

So we've got to run . . . all
we want is to run, run
and rest! . . . and run
until we've run and run
against Kelly . . . like a

Lion loose here, where
the air is like cow shit through buttermilk.

XIV

. . . Kelly (Kelley) I have run
races alright, running from
cops clanging red freight car
door to beat eight months' automatic
on the road chain gang
outside Denver . . . can
you imagine so dumb
as to be headin' into
Denver not knowing the
Railroad Detective Training
School was there and my
Olympic possibilities for
our team, old buddy, were
proven when I leaped a
fence as a boy fast enough
with my pockets full of
somebody else's Crab Apples
to beat Buck Shot headed
for my ass. Buck Shot goes
like human runners too,
there's a shot and you're off,
but Buck Shot isn't human
and so doesn't have to
breathe right or pace,
it goes directly for
the finish line and if
you're running ahead of it
and it doesn't catch you,
you ought to be up for
invitation to run in
Cummington to try to take Kelly.

XV

. . . We are seen now, the
only way to get out of this

now, humiliation of being
beaten again, to call out
loudly for all to hear
             "Just foolin' " or
"sorry!" or, "Hey, Kel . . . Kelley?
I know you ran at Wellesley
long ago . . . but did you also
come down to Maine
to Summer Camp!?"

XVI

Kelly come down Dodwells Road
so fast his Flats slapped
the dusty earth held
back on itself.
A good-natured furrowed brow
over eyes so cold I could
see Nova Scotia in them.

He took a hard look at me
and I at him, no recognition,
for time shatters features
and attitudes, but
Kelly (Kelley) has the
heart of a Roman and the
survival instinct
of a running Christian.

I look at him hard . . . is
he the Kelly? Looked like
him because I wanted him to.
If he took the heart
out of me by not being
the Kelly, he had the race,
for I am one of those who
feel always cheated by
man and opportunity.

But Kelly run up Port Hill
Road, that road in Cummington
like it's a jumping out of a

Jack-in-the-Box snake, narrow
curving straight up, he went up
like he was drawn to the top, but
I could see for myself that
nothing was helping him.

I took off and in the
heat of my anticipation
that he'd win I
made the hill too, but
the gut of my running
was pulled to its belly button hook,
and one more step would unravel me.

There was Kelly on the
far side of Gates' house
trotting, fists driving exhausts.
You saw no flame
but the way they were closed,
I knew his hands had
grabbed all the
air they'd need to pull the
big sheet world to him, which
would look like running if
you didn't know what he
was doing.

He owned the earth of running, he
is Champion Kelley.

Then he ran right through me
as though a kite
had taken air.

XVII

And now, my Father, furious
at the spilt milk of me,
life is a blend of death that
didn't finish us. I have

imagined this up to win your
heart beyond the grave.

We'll meet again and you
can tell me you love me then . . .

. . . From an old Flemish painting
did that crew creep from the Portrait again
and, as they got old Rip . . . for twenty-five years
this time, got us sleeping again . . . giving
themselves new names for us to know them
by, Hudson, Nixon . . . and one of them
Joe McCarthy . . . There are always the
Dominie Van Shaicks to give them such an
innocent place to hide as in a Portrait to
gaze down on us until we develop into
something to come out of hiding for . . . Washington
Irving, you told us where they were!

But, just where in Tarrytown . . . I know
the theories, but just where was
Van Shaick's house . . . we
must find the spot and turn it
into a national shrine of mourning, how
far from Sunnyside, Van Shaick's house!

. . . Now it's Kelly (Kelley) and
me on Cummington Berkshire
wide meadows for our ring
and the sawdust of dry
dusty road for our feet to
shuffle in as we closed and
moved to each other, me, with
the cold fear years thinking about
bad beating I took that hit
so hard at the virginity of
self-assurance as to almost
demolish it and make a life
for me of jumping every
time something clattered,
shaken, I ran scared

where God and my mother
intended I go bravely
into challenge with
endurance joy to struggle
to achieve instead of broken dread.

And now here to me came
he who hit so hard, but
the fatiguing destruction of
just surviving exhaustion
had long ago quashed my
initial fury and now here
came to me he who I had
come after in my head every
time weakness in me ruined
my pursuits, here was
some man named Kelly . . . was
he my Kelly? The anger that
furies vengeance at my
violation, which time lets
you enjoy as reason you
never risked much, so here we
stood now two old men and
me still not certain he is
"the" Kelly I want, here and
the heart of my fight gone
in the running he won winning
the lost happiness I was
looking for in taking him
and he saw it in my look
when we touched knuckles, yet,
still, the spineless animal
weakness to kill those
weaker than us, we think,
urged him to throw
his left at my nose now and
I hadn't thought he would so
didn't quite move out of the
way but was glazed along my
left eyebrow like splitting

plastic, a zipper opening,
then did I hit him with a
right I started at the
bottom of Mexico and delivered to him at the
top of the Alaska of his
jaw so he went down in Cummington,
but he had always loved the
take too, whereas I had not
liked any of it, so I
realized he had still won,
his happiness in surviving
blows as well as giving
them, nothing short of
killing him would win
for me and I wouldn't
do that and if I would
he'd be beyond feeling
what I did to him and in
the life of middle light
on the way to eternity,
outside of the flesh that
had been him, he'd look at
it, the body that had
carted him around, and at me
supposedly certain I'd
finally put an end to him,
and knowing eternal life,
would smile thinking of
my surprise on seeing him
again poised to run or
ready to throw blows
on the backside of the sun
where Mars's craters gape,
when it's my turn in the
long tunnel.

I turned to gaze on him to
see if I'd enjoy the earthly
sight of him lying on
Cummington ground, but before

I could consider whether I
would like seeing him down he
was up and jogging
and he was on flat Fairground
Road, then onto Dodwells and gone.

. . . Was he my Kelly?

Whole green
was absolutely quiet.

Like when thunder
has stopped clapping.

           Look what I did,
Father, look what I did
for you, come to
Cummington to take Kelly!

But there was a "Kelley"
Wilbur wrote of and
he took me . . . I cannot
go find what never existed . . . even
for us, Father!

Even for you and me, I am not
Warrior Knight or Athlete, but
I'm old Boppledock the apple-cheeked
kid you carried a picture of in your wallet . . .

And you, Hudson, back!
Back into your painting! I'm
wise to you and your booze.
My soul has been touched by you.
You have brushed my life
like windshield wipers separate
white snow, but the earth lust
of me still hates.

Not now, Hendrick, not quite yet!
Come into the woods with your sauce
another time. I will
drink you under table if I can
or you will put me to sleep then, but

I do not think you would let me wake again
to come out with what I know.

I don't commit the crimes you die for, the
crimes kill me. I am a victim of belief.
I recover and go on until my work is done
or my last breath is snuffed like
the palm of a hand on a candle.

Then, Father, we'll
meet again.

You can tell me you love me then.

Book II
Shatterhouse

I

Mother, we'll meet again.
I will tell you I love you then.

I went drinkin'
me, Bop, why not!

Drinkin' put me in
Little Hope Hospital.

Me, Bop, middle age now, become
like Stephen Crane characters,
"Mr. Blanc" and like the "Swede,"
almost insane in an alien environment
that does not understand him. Bop no
longer young, a furious Bop raging for
original America in fantasy Mace
and Armor seeking original American
virtue up in Cummington, Massachusetts to
do battle with and run against the great
Marathon Champion Kelley, really seeking

a boyhood Kelly tormentor . . . Now, my Mother,
America's become a nation of Peeping Toms
rather than participants. We seem to wish
to commit suicide, lost, imagination and
risk . . . lost risking, like Anthony Hecht
risking cruelty in classicism, the very
young French Legionnaire of
Hecht's "The Deodand"—where
has our Individualist like Jack London
gone, like Karl Shapiro poems, "Homo"
"Caitlin Thomas" . . . Karl Shapiro not

faculty at an Eastern College because
he stood up against Pontius Pilate's being rewarded.
. . . Almost to the end of your short life, Stephen

Crane, your whole reputation rested on manufactured
tales about things you knew absolutely nothing of,
which means you risked, took a chance, invested
yourself . . . before writing "The Men in the Storm," it
is said that you stayed up all night outdoors in a
snowstorm so that you could try to drench into
yourself through personal involvement, exposure, the
actual experience—not for really long enough to

really know what it's like to be out in the cold,
but nevertheless, we are told you did this, felt
it was necessary to experience before you wrote what
you now wanted to write . . . That was the old American!
. . . which taught you to become able, finally, to write
the greatest Western story ever written by anyone . . .
. . . Bop, thwarted, frustrated human being needing
identity, love, needing to be center of attention
who is at emotional point of needing to be
taken seriously by triggering circumstances
to become his own death, but needing someone

else, an executioner, to do it for us, drink, drugs . . .
. . . Bop very near to becoming like Stephen Crane's
Swede, finally pushing one person too many,
the gambler, gets what he most fears and yet
wants, his death—but Bop survivor discovers
it is up to us what happens. Cure lies in us.
. . . When you wrote "The Blue Hotel," Stephen
Crane, in the year you wrote it, it was startling
for probing and seeking into characters as you
dissected them, stunning, when you wrote, for a
creative writer to set a piece of writing

around a man obviously mentally ill and to show
what happened to him and the effect of it on
everyone—you were haunted all your brief life
by the dilemma every writer who is any good faces,
that of having to write about something in order
to learn to write at all, but on the other hand
constantly aware of not really knowing anything
worth telling . . . so one invests . . . one risks! . . . I

went drinkin' agin, me Bop, why not!
Drinkin' put me in Little Hope Hospital . . .
'specially after me-n-Buffer Rose

discuss what happen to his daughter, Evelyn-n-
I don' recall it all clear 'til after
I'm outa what they call Detox-n-into "Th'Community"
in Little Hope, while Mrs. Bop's thinkin' I'm havin'
a breakdown . . . duzzis soun' like th'thoughts of
a man breakin' a'course not! . . . but everythin' is
overwhelmin'. Th'whole America I love-n-unnerstood
. . . I THOUGHT I unnerstood . . . is changed.
I hope it isn't gone . . . We get up every mornin'
-n-go look th'same t'th'physical eye
like a camera only takes the surface picture.

We went from the wheel to the moon,
underneath we are sunk in addiction . . .
. . . Mother, we ran and boxed a man
for Father, for true virtue, for ideals
expressed at America's inception . . . but
we cannot correct what exists by taking on
what does not. Cure lies in us.
. . . Mother . . . I been drinkin' agin . . . I
come upon a truth about great danger in America
now for your granddaughter, Lollibop . . . Mother,
Peer pressure to dissipate, self-destruct—but

that's not what set me drinkin . . . Mother,
I was a victim who gave up, not now, Mother, no
more, but I'm tellin' you 'bout when I went
drinkin' agin before I come to see it's in me
what I become and America again once more . . . Mother,
my Mother, we'll meet when the sun sits down
on the moon and all the geese fly nowhere and
all our breath is let go . . . I'll be meetin'
Father too an' who knows maybe even Young Billy,
my only brother is sorry we never had much
to do with each other as age's sudden wisdom

watching our own children's relating to each other,
realizing we often do what our spouses wish, rather
than what we sometimes ached to do, makes Young Billy

see as I do that long before women married us, neither
of us ever had a chance with each other, who knows—
maybe his adrenalin was the sustained hatred of me,
criticism of my very existence his life preserver . . .
. . . and to like me would have broken something in him;
the end of his anger his ruin—who knows
what he needed just to accomplish growing up, he'd lost
everything I had . . . too. Brothers are not

able to pick each other . . . should I have ever
yearned for anyone to ever count on after
you left me, Mother . . . Mother, Young Billy
and me never had a chance with each other . . . maybe
I'll see him again, too, though, Mother when
the lights get too bright for my eyes, Mother,
and I close them, my last hearing,
the sea of Maine in my dying ears . . . and ocean-cold
smell come suddenly to my nose . . . Look! Sea Gulls
in fog and the stink of the clam sea as
low tide takes me out . . .

II

Drinkin' again, I found myself in
Little Hope Hospital monitored by
Staff Lucy Bubblegum and Illys of
"The Community" like Bludgeon, Motorcycle
gang mentality here to help his trial and
Toothpick In Featherhat The Farter . . . The
Bop's turned from patient payphone in the
hall as Bop saw Lucy Bubblegum stepping
out of Staff room and in a low well
controlled functioning-in-society able
tone, Bop asked—"What would the proper

procedure be to request to be excused from a
Group Therapy session, not frequently, or even
twice, just once if a particular long-distance
call from New York City comes for me?" "Concerning
what!?" She chewed her gum, blank expressionless
face, cruel eyes taunting, hoping they
could cause something . . . agitate ill people off

balance, unable to fight her, her victims . . .
"Concerning what!" Mrs. Bop exploded . . . "You
mean this man is expected to tell you our
personal business!?" Bop waved his hand

to try to silence Mrs. Bop, show functioning-
in-society not getting shook by Lucy Bubblegum
since he had to stay there in Little Hope
after Mrs. left unless he signed himself
out against medical advice which wouldn't be
demonstrating how much he really wanted to
become well, and now he was beginning now to
fear. (It's too womb-warm here, warm beds
and good meals, "Staff" like aunts and Bop'd
actually been voted by fellow Illys six
"steps" his first try when he read his soul

out to them, to Bludgeon, George, Toothpick
In Featherhat The Farter, Lucy Bubblegum off
"The Orange Contract" six steps which meant
he was back on earth again among those who
could cast a vote) this wife-strife wife
tirade might cause his reevaluation . . . wife'd
leave Little Hope for real world of innocent
until proven guilty, personal privacy . . . no
need to tell anyone your personal business . . .
. . . Suddenly Boppledock's head felt like a
branding iron white-hot was cooking his skull,

it "hurt" . . . This "occurrence" could get me
reevaluated. I'd be brought up at Community
Meeting the best way being me doing it to me to
demonstrate to the Community I was aware that
in a social situation anger flared . . . Bop said
to Lucy Bubblegum who wasn't a nurse or
even a trained Psychologist, but held
his life in her grimace . . . "A man wants
to send us money to feed our child, pay
our rent while I'm in here benefiting from
all this yet unable to try to function in

society and he doesn't know how we do
things here at Little Hope Hospital, so,

to him, what his concern is liable to be
is that he's running a long-distance phone
bill from New York City and now how we do
things here at Little Hope to help people
that help has never helped before, time after
time, Little Hope after Detox Center, isn't
even known to our dear, dear friend who is
telephoning us from New York City to try to
be of help to us if he can, so, please,

Lucy (it was alright to use Staff's first
names, they encourage it and they use yours)
can you tell us the proper procedure to
request that if a long-distance telephone
call comes for me I'll be allowed to leave
whatever Therapy Group I'm in and take the
call . . . ?" Looking blank, her eyes barely
making their threat, Lucy Bubblegum said,
almost reverting to her 7th grade
self, blowing a bubble around her chew,
"I don't think that's important enough

to leave Group." (Was she just saying
this to see how me Bop'd cope with it and
in a social situation too . . . there right
in front of Bop's wife!?) "WHAT!" screamed
free wife . . . Heads of Desk Staff jerked
as one, yearning for Mrs. Bop . . . at
that moment the Barracudas would have
tossed Bop loose for her. Right there Bop
felt his control slip through his forehead.
The branding iron hot in his skull . . . "Is
there a doctor here!?" Bop heard from far

        away . . . Mrs. Bop seemed saying
        it. "This man, my Bop, Boppledock's
        having a breakdown right here in
        front of my eyes . . . " . . . Bop floating
        . . . wondering—is that what they do
        here at Little Hope, break you like
        breaking a bone to then set it
        right so it will heal right . . . is

that it . . . they want you to break
so you'll recognize yourself? . . .
. . . hey waidaminute!—(through

Bop's thinking—) I'm not crackin' she's
wrong! My Mrs.'s wrong! I'm thinkin' this
out here, duz that sound like th'thoughts
of-aman breakin'!? . . . Here-m-I thinkin'
this out while Mrs.'s callin' f'doctors . . . I'm
not breakin' but it's a wonder I'm not.
—What worryin' him flooding in him now—
what a man of his generation could never
let himself come out with at his age in
therapy . . . The drinker overwhelmed with
conceiving . . . Drinkin' with Buffer Rose,

within that Guinness Stout-n-ice-cold ale . . . I Bop
come upon a truth . . . vague like flushing and
the voices far off when you've been knocked out,
like someone's over you sayin' "He's had enough!"
. . . Mrs. Bop standin' there yellin' f'help for him
-n-that he was havin' a breakdown while through Bop
the death you die while you're alive . . . I come upon a
truth, Buffer talkin', talkin' with Buffer Rose inna bar
we come into outa his car-n-it was my "shout" too,
but Buffer alright, he buys! We're
talkin'-n-suddenly what we're sayin'

is about th'great danger of these times
my little Lollibop lives in . . . Lollibop
-m-only child, her girlfriend, Evelyn,
Buffer Rose's daughter only 13 on Cocaine,
drink . . . They've put her every place, don't
do no good, them no help f'children hospitals,
Deciduous Hills-n-Shortshift, Coniferous Reaches—
. . . only place left Evelyn hasn't fallen in yet,
is th'last try children's hospital, Abuse . . . strike
horror inna young child's heart, they cut your
hair off there, make you go every place in diapers

so Evelyn been bein' good, takin' maybe only one hit
when her knees banjo if she don't . . . she gettin' it,
Buffer suspect, from one a th'high school custodians,

who couldn't get laid f'himself . . . Buffer find him
he be walkin' on his elbows . . . but th'real thing makin'
Buffer-n-Charlene Rose mad, th'new school of Psychologist
says to Buffer-n-Charlene, Evelyn not a victim of
Statutory Rape even if Pinhead th'sailor who fucked her
four or five times, a 30-year-old man did come before
custodian-n-he diddled her tit nipples hard 'til
they send shortwave messages, a 30-year-old grown man

arouse sensual ache to be fulfilled in
her so she come back agin-n-agin f'more of
this jest wunnerful thing! . . . yet Buffer
tell me he sit in Coniferous Reaches hospital
where children go, listenin' to a male
Psychologist look him right inna eye-n-tell
him that he knows th'law don' agree with him but
he does not feel what Buffer's daughter Evelyn
participate in is "rape," he consider it rape
only if girl is forced . . . in other words
Evelyn age 13, seduce th'grown man . . . men.

Wimmen responsible f'all sex! . . in other
words th'fuckin' of a naturally curious
adolescent 13-, 14-year-old child not by another
13-, 14-year-old child but by a grown man
is not to this Psychologist Statutory Rape
-n-I'm about t'really go drinkin' agin when
I'm hearin' another thing wrong with America,
not clearheaded enough to think, it isn't
jest in America sumthin' like this'd be wrong,
-n-that isn't what should be concernin' me but
what attitude has come to in my country.

-n-I'm about t'go really drinkin' when I'm hearin'
this from m'old buddy Buffer . . . I
went drinkin' . . . Nobody's fault . . . A
drinker can't blame anyone. Cure lies in us
I jest couldn't stop. I didn't want to . . .
You must want to. I'm inna situation lissenin'
t'Buffer Rose who come over got me at my house
before Mrs. Bop got home from her steady-payin'
good job as a Parole Officer . . . Buffer get me to

a six-pack of ice-cold ale in his car, sippin'
while he's tellin' me about Evelyn, he, Buffer th'biggest

fucker you ever saw of anythin' with a hole
cryin' his insides out when it's his Evelyn
we talkin' 'bout got fucked . . . prob'ly got taught to
suck it too, though neither Buffer or I say that
right out, 'though once that all me-n-Buffer
like, though 'course y'd never marry a girl who
would-n-til that Deep Throat come out inna movies
y'wondered how y'd ever bring sumthin' like that up
t'Mrs.-n-never dared to . . . Y'd hint, but one look
from Mrs. Bop-n-I never suggest it agin-n-I don't think
Buffer did either . . . Y'd say to Mrs. . . . we oughta go

check out what's Deep Throat . . . but one look from Mrs.
. . . we had to make it on our memories . . . Now here-m-I
sippin' agin with m'memory, at this same time I'm
th'Father of 15-year-old Lollibop-here-m-I Bop rememberin'
girls I took inna car's back seat, took 'em out for no
other reason, me 14, with my ass beat so hard at home
by Housekeeper I had to fuck for my
very survival cock weapon and savage into girls.
Th'girls loved it, I keep tellin' m'self now . . .
Loved it, waited for us to come in our car every
Thursday night when we'd drive-n-do it-n-go

dancin'-n-do it again 'fore we took 'em home
but way deep in me was a dirty feelin'-n-I'd
laugh nervous like it would go away if you
jest went ha ha ha ha w'd drown out, throttle
th'awful feelin' you were a coward only offerin'
a girl a good time if she'd put out . . . It was
a frightenin' feelin' of self-digust . . . yet
lust come back-n-you'd do it agin-n-agin-agin . . .
Laughin' thinkin' of Roberta-n-how I
had her turned around on her hands
-n-knees and took her whisperin', plunged

in whisperin' inner ear thisis how everybody do it . . .
. . . cold sweat, Bop memory . . . victim vengeance memory
now not wantin' it t'ever happen t'Lollibop knowin'

y'gut it cummin'f'whut y'done.
Bop drinkin' . . . Everythin' overwhelmin' . . . America
I loved-n-unnerstood . . . where!?, where is it!?
Mother, we'll meet again. I will tell you I love you then.
. . . for carrying little constantly shitting me
around in your arms all the time as long
as you could. Crude as I turned out, whatever
softness, grace, compassion, courage I have is

from your cuddling me and talking to me, telling me
you loved me although I don't remember it. I know it.
I know you did . . . Mother, when we meet I will tell you
I love you for my first years walked by you, talked to
by you, instilled with the only love I ever knew but
it was enough to clip the mass murderer in me . . . Mother . . .
. . . I went drinkin' agin, me, Bop . . .
Screams somewhere in the boozing.
Drink with anyone . . . Hobozo mass
murderer, old friend, doesn't matter.
The neon's on. The bottles are splashing

your soul into the dark corners of calm
doom . . . He's got a quart, I've got a
dollar. We put the town under beer suds . . .
Wandering on the slippery peeling
to bars to someone's house. Sitting
hunched over wet brown bags in
freezing somebody's car vulnerable
to be knifed or suffocated and vanished
for the ale-stained cash loose in shirt
pocket or crumpled around keys. Worse
horror is you live and do not die when

you are numb blotted on the world your
sweat tossing the water of you onto cold
day, but dry out frightened and down.
Weak and frail lost to everything. All the
faces of your drinking partners blurred in
your retching. There are no good friends of the glass.
. . . Is that it!? . . . You're not makin' it, Bop,
even here in Little Hope any more than

you made it outside in society, no you didn't!
Couldn't function again and again . . . can't
blame Lollibop, can't blame anyone . . .

>. . . Bop heard Lucy Bubblegum say, it
> seemed from far away . . . "I think he's
> handling himself well." The real
> nurses exchanged looks . . . Right there
> with wife and Lucy Bubblegum, Bop got the
> feeling nurses weren't "certain"
> same treatment's for everyone . . . Bop
> . . . bewildered staggering drunk found
> himself part of a "Community" of people
> he'd shake like fleas outside. By the time
> you leave Little Hope your face has its stamp.

III

. . . Hands reaching in through ground floor
bedroom windows and stabbing our
children to death . . . You're lying
asleep in your bed, a hand reaches in
and plunges death into your chest.
What about the unstable parents
of the child, how do you live through
your own child's call to you for help? . . . and
you came rushing . . . but the blade of the
knife had already killed her. How do
parents survive waking up out of

sound sleep to screams of their progeny
already killed but calling to you and
asking Daddy, not for Frowning Boo-Boo
the Teddy Bear, but for her life? She
knows she is dead. She's too young
to realize it. And you see the blood
spurting goodbye to you. Your own
child's blood is running away.
The red blood of your infant
is running out. Just an hour ago
she had almost a Century. Now she

does not have a minute. But you have
and how will you live the minutes
wondering over and over how you
could not have failed your child
who called out to you in her last breath?
You'll go over in your mind every evil
you ever did and convince yourself you
had this coming, just so you can live
with it . . . or you will never live with it.
You'll hit everything that moves and really drink.
Killing yourself desperately in despair.

The mother will never get over it.
No one will matter now, her baby is dead.
Yes, they'll "get" Hobozo, "he" will slip,
he undoubtedly wants to get caught, he's a
Harvard man who one day will become tired of
what he's become or get carefully careless . . .
The sneering, chortling snicker chuckling
will whimper in him; he is sick. The poor
ender of my daughter's whole life is ill and
it will be learned that it *was known* that "this"
Hobozo was very murderously dangerously available,

free . . . the tragedy will come out that he
wasn't meant to be loose on us, to get the
chance to reach in his arm through the
bedroom window of young girls with a knife
in his hand . . . and it will be learned that
in the millions of details and paperwork that
it seems to take to handle sick people, this Hobozo
was known, let out of hospital because
no one could snap a phone call about him
to anyone responsible . . . don't let this
Hobozo out, he's a killer . . . and so

young girls didn't even have a chance.
He'll reach his arm in through the
bedroom window of our young children
and stab them to death . . . yet must be
forgiven because we knew him, somebody
did . . . but it all got lost in paperwork . . .

Why does he do this . . . is there this way
to make love that orgasms by the sudden
surprise death of my child in her bed for
Hobozos stalking our nights as if their
penises are invisibly wired to knife blades? . . .

. . . Murderer stalking children to snuff
them out from pain he knows or to kill them
little before they grow hairbrush hands . . . This
Hobozo beside Boppledock in the rowboat of suds,
bought barroom companion. A flash from killing
Bop too but cunningly realizing the cover right
in front of everyone's eyes sitting and talking
and drinking free on this fat fool's coin . . . bright
Harvard graduate in self-destruction . . . He
can't stand to succeed, he's brilliant,
understands the schemes, whores

other people are, whore he is
become sarcastic in his illness,
into Soup Kitchens when he
isn't locked up to prevent
himself from himself . . . or . . . children . . .
while he bums you he senses you sense
something about him, it's in his eyes
that do not think you "see" them . . . it's
in his illness to think only he "sees"
and he is missed by everyone, by police
searching for the killer, even the

doctors who know him best and are reading
the slaughter over quick breakfast of a
fast coffee and a roll before making
rounds of the ward he should be on . . . miss
him . . . it's too true to be true . . . he is
missed until his death is done, he still
breathing blended into Soup Kitchen
naturally hidden from last murder because
none of them make sense and he's killed
and is back mopping for Father The Priest or
he cuts himself again just enough to

get committed and so psychiatrically
diagnosed as destructive to himself not
others, safe inside while the heavy
manhunt looks ruthlessly for him but
cannot find him and then he does not kill
immediately, there is a warmth, pleasure
in his Harvard brightness reading *The
New York Times* and even the *Daily News*
theory as one of half-a-hundred
in a chair in the Soup Kitchen silent or
cleverly better, mutters to himself

having him a conversation that everyone
including Police walk right by dismissing
him as the knifer. He's no one's
preconceived idea and so gets away.
He bums you as much to irritate as for
any need . . . cigarettes . . . alcohol, when
he can slink to it out of your sight
in cunning of realize you visualize him
downing wine not stabbing . . . he hides
behind laughter bitter at itself he uses
to protect himself from what Cambridge,

Massachusetts required him to realize as
our probable opinion of people with no
commitment. He drops famous names as
family friends and they well may be
friends of his family but they're
not his friends and his bitterness
is almost crying, heaving his
hurt heart into somewhat of a
foolish giggle telling you he
phoned them and they told him
to go get a job . . . that's very

funny to him, reassuring himself
in these calls, in perhaps a note
to someone home sometimes that
there's nothing for him there
if he wanted to stop the killing,

no one at home says come home. No
one wants him where he came from . . .
He laughs in your face, amused
you don't know how many children
will never grow up, excited by
what he thinks you might do in

your tearing him limb from limb it's
almost wonderful!!, the thought to him.
He is an intelligent man and no one
knows better than he what he has become.
There are moments when he is horrified,
recalls boyhood, the rage which he
had to find to survive. Survive?
Why kill strangers then, why not
the people who killed his life before
it began . . . it's all twisted in him
because . . . he loves children!

In Saint Vincent de Paul Place Soup Kitchen,
men and women look as if the day stuck to them.
Smell the rhubarb of them surviving as scavenger
or into Soup Kitchen for food, companionship.
Hobozo stalks rubbish, robber of our skeletons.
Hovering in dilapidated abandoned neighborhood
where the wino in rags fears for his life. The
dust that is left on the earth of the dead blows
away until the yesterdays of Post Cards are gone.
All the towns are run from and we are in fright
of charity. Downtown moved out of town.

IV

. . . You are someone who has not functioned
in society . . . the game here is to get you
as you come in, while you are just arrived,
confused, flipped, to "write a contract" . . . a
confession against yourself, to sign forms
so they can tell you you "agreed to" abuse,
to be ridiculed, to be judged by other Illys . . .
but they don't surround you with
liquor or Heroin the way you will

be surrounded the instant you leave
Little Hope . . . no, "theory" is you

haven't functioned in society
again and again, time after time,
so, make your life miserable with
criticism, humiliation, ridicule, which
signed forms read you say you agree to,
but the thing is you really didn't, wouldn't
have in good shape, so they're setting you
up as much as you're already set to find
drink as soon as you can again . . . Cure lies
in us. They get you to write a confession
against yourself, sincerity of which is

estimated at how much of a deceiver you
reveal you are and *maybe you* are, but the
human next to you may have really tried out
there in real world, really struggled, worked,
supported people . . . Suddenly his job world
collapsed, vanished and he is entering
middle age a weakling, admittedly, unable
to control urges, urge to shoot, urge to
drink . . . and he or she may be young in a
world with no base, no clear direction . . . Now
Bop is honest enough to write out for

them what they would not know of him to
use against his already disturbed inner
state if he did not come out and tell
them those things of battered childhood
and heartbreak he somehow survived
through day when Father would scream
"There's nuthin' Gawdam wrong with you
but y'lazy arse which I whipped with a
switch from a good birch tree I let you
pick out yourself as Gawd directed me to—
doin' m'duty by you but look whut you become!

"*Look* at you! You ain't no son a'mine! If you
do this you are on your own!" Here in Little
Hope Hospital where you'd hoped for Individual
help from somebody possibly qualified, the

idea is to irritate you so you'll "act" . . . so
you'll never want to ever come back to *this*
place! But you hardly will if you're cured . . . if
you can control your urge . . . "Making you over"
teaching you to tell on everyone, to "bring up"
in group half-overheard personal telephone
conversations, which the one you listened

in on is expected to relish "revealing" to
everyone . . . it puts a stamp on faces, creates
illness where none existed, where a Heroin
habit existed . . . where an alcohol habit existed
but where telling on someone, and yourself
was always reprehensible, now you're supposed
to because . . . because you "haven't been
interinvolving with society" . . . haven't been
able to respond, haven't been being responsible,
so "theory" here is that a Community of ill
people can judge each other, one is to be made

over, haven't been able to stay sober, cease
suicide attempt, stop th'snortin' . . . as you are . . .
now one is to become a snitch on oneself and
anyone else in "The Community" a half-overheard
telephone conversation you're having, you "thought"
privately, brought up in Community Meeting, that
from what was "overheard" by Community member Toothpick
In Featherhat The Farter, evidently you don't like
it here . . . community ill person, ill as you are and
now, here, medication crushing snorting Toothpick In
Featherhat The Farter allowed to bring up what might

be so private from your outside real world as to
do you serious damage by being made to discuss it
with people who haven't been able to function in
real world time after time, again and again . . . Bludgeon,
Motorcycle gang sodomist here awaiting upcoming trial so
good lawyer can advise court that this here Bludgeon has
changed, joined "Community Group"
hoping that Little Hope will get him
back out on th'street to "scan th'man, man! to

rob and drink and snort an' git kyik!"
sodomizing, killin', hittin', stompin', that

th'life, ye-ah! . . . in hyre, in hyre, Little
Hope a joke! Lotsa deadbeat lotsa fucks oughta
be wasted save sassiety feedin' 'em man! Now
me Blud-geon! I look inna mirror an' say
I be right back! Ye-ah! I do I do I do . . .
Bludgeon is now "makin' hissef over" Yippie!!
lak his lawyer say, man! Interactin' they
callsit with otheren peeple (he might
usually mayhem) . . . outside . . . outside a'hyre
Bludgeon in business with Toothpick In Featherhat
Th'Farter . . . Th'Fierce-White Bike Collectors whoo-whee!-n-

Toothpick In Featherhat Th'Farter's wommen Arlene
-n-Bludgeon's deary Dixie find th'word Alzheimer's
disease inna newspaper and th'other afternoon afore
Bludgeon picked up-n-his lawyer say "better be
Little Hope," this old lady she's walkin' downa street
toward her son's house an' by th'time she got to th'corner
she couldn't remember anythin' an' jes then's when
Arlene join her, poor old thing, she gets lost on buses,
lost—Arlene walk along beside her-n-within a block
ole Lady Lotte think she have a new frien' . . .
. . . Soon deary Dixie pull up by them inna car,

in minutes all three inna car. They ride aroun'.
Then Arlene tell ole Lotta she need to cash a
check f'Four Thousan' dollars . . . It from
someplace call National Auto Service, Seattle,
Washington . . . could dear ole Lotte hep them ut?
Do she have a bank nearby? Do she have money inna
bank? Yes there is an account at The Trusting Trust,
nex' stop th'bank. While Arlene-n-deary Dixie wait
inna car, dear ole Alzheimer Lotte go in her bank. A
few minutes later she come out witha deposit slip.
No no no no no, Arlene explain, there a mistake—

check not t'be deposit-t-be cashed! This time a
Teller explain t'poor bewildered dear ole Lotte
th'check cannot be cash until it clear . . . only

way to do it now would be to cash in against her life
savings account-n-she, poor dear ole Lotte's only got
Four Thousand Two Hundred dollars in her life savings
account . . . Uhhuh! Thet's how she do play! Yippie!!-n-
Bludgeon-n-Toothpick In Featherhat Th'Farter ridin'
roun' on motorcycles in full cycle rigs, roar aroun'
town tryin' t'collect money owed f'rent, bad check,
court judgment . . . Th'Throttle City Credit Collection

Bureau admire Bludgeon-n-Toothpick In
Featherhat Th'Farter . . . its records show 3.5 million
in bad checks durin' Reagan paradise-n-Bludgeon-n-
Toothpick In Featherhat Th'Farter a credit to credit
collection . . . Ridin' roun', Bludgeon he wear a
turquoise ringin his ear, a bandanna roun' his shoulder
length hair, a tattoo of a wommen's nice bare bottom
in th'flex of his arm muscle . . . Toothpick In Featherhat
Th'Farter he wear a bandanna too tied roun' his
head, leather vest unner his jacket . . . He-n-
Bludgeon look f'all th'world like they might

break your arm, but Toothpick In Featherhat
Th'Farter, he say, in High School English, they
jes' "look tough," their appearance hep th'Fierce-White
Bike Company business by encouragin' peeple
t'pay up th'money they owe . . . It Bludgeon's
idea . . . When he bounce a few checks hissef
while recoverin' from a tummy fulla knife
an' couldn't get about much, collection
agencies didn't try very hard to collect he
discover . . . but Bludgeon lak his butt fuckin'
no matter how much deary Dixie give him her

nice fat bare bottom 'cause he make her-n-thet
gettim inta trouble, gettim arrested-n-facin'
serious prison . . . Bludgeon lak a good man onceinnawhile-n-
all'ays hav' Toothpick In Featherhat Th'Farter
but Toothpick In Featherhat Th'Farter don' never
givim too much onna outside, 'less Bludgeon he
start singin' Th'Star Spangled Banner-n-talkin'
t'im 'bout th'Flag, allegiance, *then* Toothpick
In Featherhat Th'Farter all'ays givim his ass,

Toothpick a loyal patriot, all'ays go f'follow
th'leader-n-Bludgeon his leader but Bludgeon he

don' do thet much, he don' believe in nuthin' 'sides
Bludgeon he don' really never wanner put his lovely
tallywhacker in where them farts of Toothpick In
Featherhat th'Farter cum from, but Bludgeon'll
do it willin' rather than completely go without
yesindeedie . . . n-Toothpick In Featherhat Th'Farter
is th'perfect trick, sidekick . . . in hyre, now when they
in Little Hope, Toothpick In Featherhat Th'Farter
shrewd, play act like he nut in court, in fact,
Toothpick In Featherhat Th'Farter's kinda surprised
he don' feel he have t'act or do much different-n-he

all'ays is—only thing not to ever make Bludgeon mad while
they in Little Hope any more-n-deary Dixie do when
they onna outside-n-if-n-when deary Dixie out
Alzheimerin' bes' thing t'do is always let
Bludgeon do whut Bludgeon he wanna . . . th'heat
come-n-git Bludgeon who true to his loyalty
immediately involve Toothpick In Featherhat Th'
Farter, for he, Bludgeon, ain' goin' nowhere
without his screwin' business associate (it all right
deary Dixie know 'bout him-n-Toothpick In Featherhat Th'
Farter-n-thet they do whatever Bludgeon wanna-n-she

relieved! 'leas' it ainna 'nother wommen!)—Now Bludgeon
cool, now he, Bludgeon brings up in Little Hope "Group"
that he knows, Bop, your phone conversation is private but
Toothpick, hyre, en Featherhat Th'Farter . . . (who gonna
be anice piecea ass inner sheets tonight after lights out
when you can tiptoe th'corridor past them desk sucks
or jes' wouldn't be *no* good at breakin'-n-enterin' . . . he,
Blud-geon good at "enterin' " alright . . . all'ays easy with
this cocaine-snortin' squealer chicken sucker, th'blade
of a small penknife right on Featherhat Th'Farter's vein
in his neck while he worked his legs up onto his shoulders

and plunged in "smop" in, chug, chug, not a sound outa
  Featherhat,
he know who fuckin' him . . . what go down in Little Hope-n-
  what

don't) . . . Now it time to mess up a few weirdo lose 'em
some "steps" except that fat gray man, that Bop, he alright!
He "regular" come roun' talk "decent" t'Blud-geon lak he know
who Bludgeon! Still gotta back Toothpick en Featherhat th'Farter
. . .
. . . Now y'phone conversation . . . Farter say he hear you tellin'
somebody how this place f'nuts-n-junkie . . . and without
   blinking
you better be able to churp to "Group" something! You know,
   Bop
. . . make it up . . . This is just some more
hustle . . . what you have to do in real

world too . . . lay it brother! . . . like
how the person on the other end of the phone
was maybe Long Time Charlie who did 7
years' hard time for driving someplace
drunk and runnin' over somebody who didn't
die and liquor caused his action because
he wouldn't have done it otherwise, just
being 3 days out right now from 5 he
done for slippin' in a liquor store with
a thirty-eight goin' off just as
twirling red bulbs drive by . . . and he's

been begging you pleeze, Boppledeck, by all
th' saints that luvya and all *that* "Staff"
almost vomits hearing . . . pleeze, Bop, turn
yourself into a wonderfully psychiatrically
oriented hospital and that's what you
were telling him you had! Now "Group"
beams at you. George, a middle-ager with
boozer forever etched in his look, looks
at you and it's three oranges time! "I
haven't liked you, Bop, from the first
second you came in here, now I do."

. . . There's dead silence. This is
Little Hope working! See! See! See what
"Staff's" been trying to tell you happens
when, when you tell the truth and come out
with pure interrelating!! . . . It's *wonderful*!!!

George didn't like you, now he likes you!!!
and it was all because Toothpick In Featherhat
The Farter took a chance at offending you,
intruded on your privacy? . . . maybe! maybe! but
you *shared* and now look at Farty! (His sneak
eyes don't know what they see, so Staff

tells him) and Bop gets up, looks sheepish,
crosses and shakes George's hand and Blu-dgeon
looks at Bop with admiration . . . "Boy do dat dude
lay down a good rap!" . . . Bludgeon naturally loves
anyone who gets out of things, especially if
he's been "set up" like he and Toothpick In
Featherhat The Farter just tried to cost
Bop "steps" if they could . . . now
AA Counselor nodding approval, looking
around at everyone, see, see what's
happening right here now this instant!?

"See the reason for 'Group,' see how we
share and tell and get well!? Boppledock's
shared with us even what everyone in the
room knows was a *private* telephone
conversation, but," her head looks like it's
turning a circle on her neck, "nothing's
private here, got to give all that over to
Little Hope Hospital" . . . We know what's best!
Your face everyone will "see" when you
leave us may have a look on it of having
witnessed some head-on collision, your

natural instinctive makeup so worked on by
us that the "look" in your face is sickness to
anyone outside in outside real world who
does not know what you were like when you
came in to Little Hope after being unable to
function in society again and again, time
after time . . . You will look cracked, even
barely able to hold yourself together
to *them*—to *them*! But they aren't *you*,
weren't you, were they!!? You are better able
to try not to ever do those things

again that brought you here, aren't you!?
. . . our "theory" here is that a "Community"
of ill people can "spot the con" everyone's
always lived by, in each other, one is to
become a snitch on oneself and anyone
else . . . tell tell tell! Accusation is
enough to get reevaluated by your
ill patient "community" and "Staff," no one
even "has to *see* something," like your
climbing out the window of your room
to smoke or go to nearby liquor store . . .

So old Bop has a week he's paying for
wasted of what was supposed to be therapy
helping *him*, while Bludgeon and Toothpick
In Featherhat The Farter twist "Group's"
honor theory system of "confessing," fellows
who have hurt people for heroin . . . When
Bludgeon and Toothpick In Featherhat The
Farter went out a window, who knows, to
suck a roach under a tree in wild bronc
moonlight, drink, who knows, and got back
inside Little Hope without being "seen"

no one "actually saw" them, Toothpick In
Featherhat The Farter had to go "tell"
Suicidal Lucille . . . here, too, at
Little Hope are those who "say" they
attempted suicide . . . If you yourself
were "well" you'd "see" that here
at Little Hope none of the light bulbs
are covered up or closets of cleaner
padlocked, many ways anyone could cut
out their life or swallow it, this
isn't any deep lockup . . . Little Hope

irked Suicidal Lucille who looked at you with
agate eyes with strange lure in them,
like being excited by the dead or
sniffing scent long gone, like
"nobody'll ever have *me*," serenely smiling
telling in Group how the first try

was the hardest, every other gets
easier and easier . . . Suicidal Lucille
felt "honor bound" to "tell Group" that
Bludgeon and Farty had slipped out of
Little Hope for a taste . . . Instantly

Mr. Adrenalin, Doc Prune's Business
Manager, whispered like a deaf undertaker
that Community Group is not a democracy,
not a place of innocence, innocent until
proven guilty . . . the brave patient who would
march against KKK better stick to his
Librium here . . . Now here's Bop in a situation
where nobody "saw" anyone go out a window . . .
. . . only Suicidal Lucille who hates Bludgeon
and Farty for what their kind have done in
her briefs . . . no one "saw" anyone go out a window

and climb back in or drink or suck or snort and
"Staff" says if whoever did it "had any guts"
they'd come right out and tell on themselves
and right here is the big flaw in Little
Hope "theory" . . . because "telling" will
not result in "hoo-ray reward" the gift of a
"step," "congratulations" for having slipped
but owning up . . . no, telling will result in
"re-evaluation" to "zero" from "step" "14"!?
Only the *very* ill will do *that* to themselves . . .
. . . not Bludgeon or Toothpick In Featherhat The Farter.

V

Poor dear lovely tiny Irish lady
trying to figure out why her
husband went to work the day she
almost killed herself, that to him
it was like any other day he had to
go out and support them, until she
looked so bad to him he brought her
to Little Hope hoping . . . one who can
still cry, still break into tears,

perhaps can be turned from what is
true, she *is* suicidal . . . the small

Irish lady, such a beautiful lost
tiny thing who talks hesitatingly
. . . "I told him I was suicidal before
we got married! I told him and yet
he went to work that day just the same!
We had our extension phone put in our
bedroom" (she's painting the air with
her fingers) . . . "That was my life line" . . .
(reflectively gazing into herself . . .
no one else but her was here in the
room now, no one else sick here) . . . "He
still went to work that day."—"My name's
Bop," I spoke up and asked . . . "You mean to
tell us that because you told him you
might kill yourself before he married
you, that means he's supposed to
always be around waiting for it or
to stop you, how could he do that
and stay sane!?" . . . "No, no" she
cries and real tears come, then
tossing her head defiantly . . . "I've
told him not to come to visit here,

not to call me on the telephone or
come until I've worked it out just
what I think of him" . . . I said
(You're supposed to give feedback in
"Group" or you can't get your "steps"
in Community vote) . . . "What you've
just said sounds like a child who's
angry at a spanking and being sent
to bed without supper because she
told her mother she's liable to
steal cookies after school, just before

supper" . . . "No, No!" she sobs, jumps up
and dashes out of the room and because
"Staff" knows you aren't going to

endure this "patient-curing-patient"
theory, the specific personal attack,
insult, criticism called "making you
over" to make you "see" you as you never
"saw" you before, but are going to
sign yourself out against medical
advice from Little Hope; because old
Boppledock, son of Mama and Dad who

flapped their way through th'20s
is going back into the fight real life is,
now "Staff"—though always up to now they've
marked down whether you've "participated"
in "Group" or not, given positive or
negative "feedback": now the half-trained
observer who oversees "Group" savagely
attacks you, because you're leaving and if
he can make you break down you'd "see" for
yourself you're in no condition to go back
to real life . . . and then he can give you

love, even his admiration, even commend you
in "Group" and to Charge Nurse and to "Staff"
but not *now*! Not *now*! Not with you doing
what you're going to do, go back to real
life realizing that cure lies in ourselves . . .
or in us with Psychiatrist and you getting at
your disturbance, not here in the open tomb
Little Hope Hospital . . . When the little Irish
lady, so tiny, so pretty, comes back
into the room from "you just don't
understand us suicides" and you

apologize publicly to help group of
Illys hear you say you're sorry, you
didn't mean to drive her to leave the
room, were only responding to her as
everyone there has felt quite free to
lay on you whatever vicious remarks
occur to them, and some were very good,
true, helpful because you wish to see

yourself get well . . . and because you
meant the poor woman no harm . . . but
half-trained observer really jumps you.

A week ago he would have pursed his
lips pained expression told you you
should do a lot of listening, after
all, you haven't been able to function
in society again and again, time after
time . . . you should do a lot more listening
than talking . . . Then a week ago he
would have soothed . . . "but you
made some good points!! good good
for involving!" and he would have asked
weeping suicidal . . . "What do you think

of Boppledock's statement? Are you
angry because your husband wasn't
right there just the day you
might have killed yourself?" She's
not even listening . . . She doesn't
comprehend anyone in the room . . . not
Toothpick In Featherhat The Farter, not
Bludgeon, not Boppledock, not Suicidal
Lucille . . . She doesn't "realize" that
half-trained observer has savagely
gone after Bop because he's not

going to endure this anymore . . . "Su-suppose
I just didn't bother to pick up the
telephone that noon . . . when he called me.
We were laughing and I giggled . . . but
suppose I just didn't answer the phone . . ."
She's furious because she is now allowing
herself to feel that he went to work
either not really caring for her, loving
her or worse, not believing she'd do it
and she's in here in Little Hope Hospital
because she got herself worked into a

state that he saw she might do it and so did
the best he could think to do then,
brought her to Little Hope . . . So what

happens to you, dear Bop, even
to Toothpick In Featherhat The
Farter . . . to toothpick-chewing
cocaine-medication-snorting Farty-
Featherhat . . . is you're here
for help, beginning to crack so
everyone's "noticing"—to find
yourself not getting "individual"

attention to what your specific
illness may be . . . First you're
in "Detox" in alcoholic's irrational
self-pity, unable to "realize" clearly,
then soon as your blood pressure and
heart lower and slow, in a "program"
of patients set upon each other,
"Community" of Illys who could
vote against what you really need
easily, since they, too, are sick, haven't
been able to function in society

again and again, time after time, so
injure you, you injured by this "patient-
curing-patient" theory therapy, you
become worse than when—when you got
to Little Hope's group of many kinds
of ill people called "A Community"
of Manic Depressives, Suicidals,
Addicts, even Motorcycle gang
mentalities here now to help
themselves in court whether
Bludgeon and Toothpick In

Featherhat The Farter do or do not tell
on themselves, the accusation against
them is believed by "Staff," by Mr.
Adrenalin, by Lucy Bubblegum . . . Bop
saw the street gang run the place
while Social Worker stuttered . . .
Lucy Bubblegum glared . . . and those who
had rammed Little Hope Hospital down
Bop sat perplexed . . . it happened

in the middle of the night, like a Billy-Jo
romance . . . "Daddy don' blow his arse away

we gonner shoot her-oin" kind of thing . . .
Toothpick In Featherhat The Farter's girl
Arlene told him no more! Goo-bye!
Bludgeon c'd have him, that dunnit!
T'hell with Little Hope, Toothpick In
Featherhat The Farter now his ole sef,
he had to git out unner a prairie dog
sky agin now, not later, now and
Bludgeon betteren not thinkin' he goin'
t'be on top all th'time no more, no sir!
Thinking this, deciding this excited

Toothpick In Featherhat The Farter and
Blud-geon like aggression, *sometimes* . . . how
you goin' t'feel gooud-n-enjoy whut y'do
t'someone you know, make 'em do 'less you
know whut it feel like an' so no one in
Th'Thrillers motorcycle gang or th'Fierce-White
Bike Company c'd ever say, Bludgeon he "do it"
but couldn't "take it!" . . . only thang y'cain't "take"
is bein' murdered ahaha! Yippie! Bludgeon he
snuck to liquor store and now in "Group"
Lucy Bubblegum looking at Bop and beautiful

tiny Irish lady with vomit in her bland head,
is excited by Bludgeon and Toothpick In
Featherhat The Farter . . . They're at least
"honest," HONEST!!? . . . well at least they're
who they are! Lucy Bubblegum senses a vague
groin ache like lust is the spoils of violence . . .
. . . "Do it to me . . .!" . . . always the music in our
secret thoughts . . . She is drawn by a cruel
line in Bludgeon's lip and his eyes
darting, finding Lucy Bubblegum
breathing hot in Little Hope . . .

VI

Father, Bop is wandering! Washington
Irving, you struck our vein, we are

narcoleptic and love fantasy . . . ghost
stories and cheap romance while we
pull covers up over our heads, the
dead calling to us the American
dream is ending . . . now our government
thinks the worst of people . . . no
longer in America, my Father, is there
belief people will do well out of love . . .
. . . we must go find our original wish

in the Cosmos and in ourselves . . . Stephen
Crane, by creating yourself in "The Blue
Hotel" as the character called "The
Easterner," "Mr. Blanc," like blank, no
mark on this guy, the Easterner, the
Easterner a person who is empty, untouched . . .
. . . Could "The Easterner" (Stephen Crane) be
telling us that all his brief twenty-eight-year
life he is not a participator . . . never served
in The Civil War or wandered New York
City's Bowery . . . things he wrote about . . . but

finally near his end, finally participated,
involved, invested himself, his soul in his dream? . . .
. . . Blanc means white, then . . . whitewash?—Peeping
Tom standing back from . . . is what Americans are . . .?
Stephen Crane come to John Donne realization when,
finally as his character The Easterner confronts the
Cowboy in "The Blue Hotel" and tells him that they each
and every one of them, all of them were responsible for
the death of The Swede . . . What of America is guilty of Bop
death if Bop was not a struggler, now, Boppledock, your son,
Father, wanders through living in swallows of blackout.

Mother, you died on me and left me.
I always thought you'd be back . . . when I
was Eight I did. When I was Nine I did. You
were just away with another boy who needed
you more than I did . . . Mother, we are each
other! You and I are each other! . . . and I
have never forgotten you, even though your
face is just a vague flash smiling up

at me when I was only seven and Big Billy
brought Young Billy and me to see you in
your hospital bed because in your dying

delirium you'd asked him to let you see us
once more. I really didn't understand that
this was the last time I was ever going to
see you and when Big Billy came to the
bottom of the backstairs below our bed-
room and called up to us that you wouldn't
be coming home (he couldn't come up to
tell us, to hold us and tell us, he had to
call the news up to us) . . . Somehow Young
Billy seemed to comprehend it, age only
six, he burst into tears, but I was too

dumb and too numb to comprehend and you
died two days before Christmas so no one
knew what to tell me with Christmas and
Santa Claus joy just about to come, so,
someone looked at Big Billy, an aunt, a
sister of yours, and I wasn't wondering
why everyone was there, Big Billy sisters
and your sister, even if it was Christmas,
never that I can remember had so many
of my aunts and uncles and their children,
our cousins, everyone been there at

Christmas before, of course I was only
Seven and dreamed a lot, got lost in my
thoughts—even then, but I wasn't wondering!
. . . *why* so many people were there . . .
and suddenly Big Billy put us with a
family who lived across the street, it
was all so puzzling, wasn't it Christmas
and weren't we going to have Christmas in
our own home . . .? I watched my chance and
I escaped, I got by whoever in the neigh-
bor family was supposed to be keeping an

eye on me and Young Billy and I ran to
my house, the house Young Billy and me
were supposed to be in and I got by an

empty kitchen into a dining room to half-
closed parlor doors and I slipped in and
there was an odor of purple violets like
in no air and there you were lying down
with your hands folded on your chest,
like you were asleep, so it was always
easy for me to believe that you'd gone
away to take care of a little boy who

needed you more than I did because I knew
I have to lie down and go to sleep! I had
seen you asleep! Suddenly bursting people
all around me and I knew I'd done something
wrong, but no one touched me, everyone
seemed to want to see what I was going to
do, well, once I'd seen you, Mother, I went
back to the neighbor's family blissfully
and I always gave it to Big Billy, he made
a Christmas for us then, no matter what
was going on in his heart.

Mother, you and I have never parted. We
are always each other . . . but men and
women are at strategy with each other
devising ways to manipulate . . . maleness,
femaleness—strategies of reproduction
differing in psychology and structure,
each pursuing differently the achievement
of life . . . The danger to love is if the
act is considered a favor women perform
for men . . . even when women are believed
to get more pleasure . . . We are strangers,

Mother, in our very sex, for while I work
seriously and hard to undo the male chauvin-
ism inbred in me as my male right, all the
while, still, the truth is that the best way
to maximize your genes' representation in
the next generation was to lay Big Billy!
Look! I am *you*, Mother. I want to be you.
We are each other. Yes, I'm many people and
I talk, sometimes slang, like when I'm with

Buffer Rose inna bar-n-we're discussin' . . .
I've many voices and I'm many people and so

is everyone, if they'd only realize it, Mother!
I've been promiscuous. I've done some filthy
things. I'm a human being! I'm not sorry
any more than you are for picking Father,
exactly! for "behind choosy" who you let
give you the seed of me. I want to be you,
Mother, I want to live the life robbed from
you young for you . . . I was worth bearing to
you, Mother, because you knew I carry half
your genes . . . The price men pay for being
spared pregnancy is the possibility the

child isn't his, no—I do not believe Big
Billy did not think I am his son, it's the
way you two did it and then had to get
married because I was in you, Mother, and
Big Billy had no choices under those day
codes and while forever and always exclaiming
"What a swell girl" you were, he never forgave
me, Mother—I changed his secret desire's
course—he had planned to fuck and run!—I've
done it myself, Mother, but in a different
time . . . Mother, Father "didn't realize his

mind." "Minds that want what the male wants
are the kind we're likely to find if we look"
—as Edwin Osborne Wilson notes—"because
that's the kind of mind whose genes get
multiplied the most"—And Osborne reminds
"We should realize that a mind like ours,
which evolves by selection is constructed
to promote the survival of the genes that
created it,—not to understand itself!"—When
I was Fourteen alone in my room, my bedroom,
your room, it had been your room when you were

a girl in that house and it was my room, I used
to almost think that I smelled you in it. Once
I swear you appeared to me there in the black

dark and told me, whispered to me to always be a
good boy . . . and I knew I would be deep in me if
I hadn't had all those beatings from nineteen-
year-old Housekeeper that broke me like
thread, everything become so overwhelming
for me forever, but I swear, Mother, that
you came to me in that room that was my
bedroom that had been your room, when I was

fourteen and you asked me to be a good boy
and I knew I hadn't been being very good, out
into every girl I could, because I was
big now and nineteen-year-old Housekeeper
was being careful but I was getting even
with any and every girl I could get back at
and then coming back into my room and
"making believe" I was with you and you were
with me . . . Suddenly I looked away from the
ceiling, there, lying there on my back on
my bed which had been your bed when my

bedroom was your bedroom and I stared at
your old wallpaper and from way in me
a deep, deep having lost someone came up
through my throat. I knew! Suddenly one
afternoon in the year that I was fourteen
that you wouldn't ever come back to me,
Mother—Big Billy always took us to visit
where they say you lie, on your birthdays,
then take Young Billy and me out to eat—
—so in this celebrating of your birthday
you were always visualized, never forgotten,

I'll give Big Billy that, he did love you
within his illness, his perpetual blessing
himself when he wasn't wiping yukky runny
fried egg from his "I must be appeased" chin
frothing, always frothing, raging at how life
had outwitted him the time he snuck you away
Mother from the family Christmas sing-around-
the-piano when he had come with my aunt who

thought she was going to marry him until I
materialized in you, Mother, but Big Billy did
love you, it fitted his romance, the one about

how God took you from him because of what he
did, Mamma!—He foisted all his professed
love of any child of his upon Young Billy who
needed love, too, and found himself doing just
about anything Big Billy seemed to want him to,
until, finally, I never saw a man absolutely
hate even the memory of his father the way
Young Billy hates Big Billy because to have
Big Billy's love, Young Billy had to give his
very personality, it's a wonder he survived!
Thank God, he did, Mother, Young Billy did

survive and you can be proud of him, Mother—
What slop!, soap opera!—It's "American," though,
and absolutely true . . . We are a nation in our
adolescence, still, over two hundred years old!
Our enemies go crazy that we survive in our
cherubic simplistic idiocy . . . Mother, I would
look at your name chiseled in stone and not
believe it . . . You were really away taking care
of a . . . I wanted you so much, Mother. You
weren't in that earth, Big Billy kept taking me
to and showing me . . . but suddenly I knew you

really were, Mother! . . . One afternoon in the
year that I was fourteen I knew that you were
dead. But I couldn't say it, even whisper, even
in a whisper to myself. I couldn't say it . . . You
were dead, not just away, but gone, oh, God!
so I am trying to write you a triology, to leave
something of us on this earth when I too breathe
no more, a trilogy, Mother, of flesh and bleeding,
not always pretty, and I was not always the good
boy I have always believed you asked me to be,
there are those who would tell you that I am not

now a real man, that I have never been a real man
and that I will never be a real man. I know I am

broken, but a coward, no, Mother. I would die as
well as most do, which is not very well. Why, I
might even be Nathan Hale on a scaffold but
won't seek one to prove it, thank you! Who
knows until their final minute shines how
they'll go out? . . . I am the best and the least
of mankind . . . but, Mother, I am the struggler
and survivor you made me cuddled in your arms.
Now what I become lies in me . . . And Father,

you and I must find each other . . . this little
country that became vast, where common men got
told for the first time in rememberable history
they had a right to the pursuit of happiness
and have not been able to handle it . . . Greed
always takes purity's place. American: He made
a motor to pull four wheels faster than two
hundred horses—beat gravity after eons lifting
flying tons into the sky and even through
very Heaven . . . He is even able to obliterate his
very trace and this earth burned-out ball float

forever as if ideas and lust and dreams
and desire never existed and no one left
to see where the burned-out ball goes
frighteningly floating . . . Now, Boppledock,
your son, Father, wanders vague through living,
drinking at success, risking freedom . . . every
once in a while a shudder of recall through him . . .

. . . once he went up to take a race
in Cummington . . . he come outa th'service, see,
and was down at th'V.A. when he picks up this
book a'po'try . . . it's been squeezed,
crumbled up some pocket "Walkin' t'Sleep" or
sumthin' . . . by somebody named Wilbur . . . and he
"thought" he seen John Wayne tellin' Ward Bond
what to do so he went up there, you know, once more
to find the original dream, to run, fight
some Kelly, Kelley? . . . was th'opponent's
name Kelley!? . . . but it never happened, it

was all just a poem . . . who reads poems . . . he
couldn't make Comanches for John Wayne to
shoot the eyes out of so they'd have to

wander between th'four winds forever and
never see God, even in his head, like horror
hangover, this Kelley, Kelly? this runner
come down Dodwells Road and beat him . . . everything
beat Boppledock . . . Father . . . my Father . . . I,
your son, Boppledock was born in the dawn of
Margarine, old tires lying like lifesavers
all over front yards, scraggly grass strangled
in mud and cars with parts missing up on
blocks rusting. Even the breathing were dead in
their futility . . . Boppledock, Depression Era baby,

son of Mom and Dad who flapped their way through
th'20s like money would never end and when it
did in bleak 30s all opportunity took a walk
to war plants ten years down the road of selling
the seat off your own toilet door-to-door for
bread in poor man's gravy made out of flour in
bubbling water in hot pan with grease. It was the
dawn of Margarine, white like lard,
disgusting looking with a little
bag of yellow color that you mixed
and mixed and told yourself tasted

like butter . . . Lucky to have it. The
air was mean . . . Father, I am your son,
Boppledock, and I will tell you I love you
when we meet . . . I didn't do any better
than you with all my complaining, all
my forever everything's your fault, never
does there ever seem to come a point
where it is my fault not your fault!
Father, I have whined myself out of whining.
Failure, finally, is your own fault, it was
never really your fault, Dad, except for

being dumb of my child abuse . . . yet all
experience turns on kinds of insights one might
never have otherwise. Who knows what's "good" or

"bad" . . . the sheltered who cannot function once
Mother and Dad vanish or the abused who can never
hold anyone close, feel warmth, give love? I know
this—we have a country, my Father, that was hard
won by common men and must not be taken by the
rich from us . . . I cannot say to you, my Father,
provider of my three meals every day
and my bed every day and Christmas

every year for almost twenty years
that I do not love you. I yearn for
my own child's love. What can I say
to you . . . ! I was Depression Era baby
born when money would never end and
when it did . . . young nineteen-year-old
Housekeeper, underpaid by stingy Dad
who blessed himself as if that forgave it.
Nobody else had to live, though, Father
you were one of the very few who could
hire anyone when mother died leaving me

to nineteen-year-old Housekeeper just
growing up out of terror of spanked childhood
herself, now raged her vengeance for being
abused on *you*, Boppledock, middle-age drunk . . .
wandering in a sea of Guinness Stout out of
Little Hope . . . she had your pants down as
often as look at you, maybe thrilled by
your humiliation with lust become mean nasty
erotic to make your bare bottom red for what
she had to do across automobile front seats
dodging the stiff stick shift to get a boy to

take her dancing and he'd put his boot
up you quick as look at you if you
so much as looked at him as you asked his
Sunday afternoon blowjob for something
to eat. He'd come to see her with nothing
better to do and for ego relief that
something of his worked in these times,
getting her with his flesh for a
woman putting him on earth, he almost

guaranteed your ass would pay for it,
throttling her life hole with his lifegiver

was better than kicking tin cans down
a dirt road or standing around some car
with its rod thrown, angry he couldn't
make it drive. He most likely walked into
auto-tire-strewn yard, bleak, lonely, awful in
its hot destitute silence . . . hot without money.
No Television then. Hot sun in no noise . . . except
maybe far off a radio singing Ruth Etting . . . Hot
day seeming to take forever to end and become
nightmare night into day never coming to an
end and you Boppledock's been stuck on her to

watch, only a brutalized child herself, a "girl" at
that, not "important," not her father's son! A girl
he'd ruined. One day in, say, late April when she
was just a little girl, she did something like
come down to breakfast late, or she
didn't get home from school on time or
left dirty clothes all over her
room and "Old Stonington" th'Sea Captain her
father, yanked her like a Raggedy Ann to
front parlor window and forced her to look
across street at Fire Chief Marston's

house while Sea Captain, "Old Stonington,"
her father, told her that when the Circus
came to town in July, he wouldn't take
her he'd take Fire Chief Marston's
little girl and all Spring passed
in its sweet smells while she
hoped against sinking-heart dread
that he didn't mean it but to Sea Captain,
"Old Stonington" this cruelty would "make"
a woman out of her, hard and knowing what
life's like . . . was better than having to

order her four hundred lashes for
disobeying him until she was split-skinned
dead and he'd have to go round steely-eyed
staring straight ahead, nobly concealing

his sorrow . . . he was what they call a
good man according to his lights and in July
when the clowns came for little children's hearts,
Sea Captain, "Old Stonington, Connecticut," her
father, kept his word . . . So young Housekeeper
she turned cold to any other child's cry,
in fact inflicted it . . . and actually expected

30 years later, Boppledock would, as an
adult, accept her explanation of how she
almost turned him stalker, unable to ever
hold anyone close, robbed of joy, life
happiness of personal involvement with
anyone or anything but bare survival, lost,
dumped through depression years into slaughter . . .
she, a "girl" screamed at to bring her father,
"Old Stonington," Sea Captain his hot bisquits
and baked beans while her brothers and everyone
beamed what a good idea it was she could take

dead mother's place, cooking, washing, waiting
on Pa every way but in bed; she had a prick to
deal with every way you look at it, kicked out by
"Old Stonington," Sea Captain, her father to baby-sit
for whatever she could get . . . into the great American
Depression. The air was mean. Children were to be "seen"
and not "heard." It was a miracle anyone ever
grew up . . . But Father, our final binding
love is I am mingled with your unfulfilled
wish to become again the original and to
make a future, your wildest imagining!

Book III
The Clear Blue Lobster-Water Country

        I

    . . . Bop's thoughts spinning in
    shot flashes . . . Central America's
    America t'be in, Bop tried

    to reassure himself now lying near
    buzz of voices . . . Father . . . Bop
    . . . vaporized!?

Mrs. Bop's face
embossed on some
clinging cliff?

Charred skin hanging off bones,
eyes hanging out . . . Lollibop
melted among roaches . . .

    . . . our dead parents' voices
    come out of our mouths . . .
    . . . Lolli, I wish

    I'd spent more time
    with you . . . am I like Big Billy, was
    he like The O'Dock . . .?

My Grandfather, Michael The O'Dock,
rushed with his hand clutched
in his mother's to escape

potatoes grinning black in their cores
and the Irish walking dead in their
own land. Dole or work

never come for those who counted
on a life of spuds. It was to
America The O'Dock came.

    Again the sea spews
    barely believing humans
    for America's one more chance.

These new among us
busy finding roof,
food, new start

are not oblivious to
possible pop that
would boil the ocean,

think of it! Glutton lobster
sneakin' along to sit on
some Mussel to eat it gulping

cooking right there in its own
seaweed, right there turning
orange in its bubbles

not up outa trap into
steamin' pot but
in its own sea.

Life's breath snuffed, cold, even
th'Moon gone, teeth chattering
in your broiled skull.

II

I was over to th'university because
Lollibop told me I ought t'learn more
'bout different worlds, not

be a Boppledock all m'life! . . . though
jest what she means by that I
couldn't figure . . . I went

t'th'university-n-met fine people
who work with *Hands Off Central America*
-n-I went over to th'university

to learn 'bout other countries without
ever bein' in any a'them, it's maybe
called fightin' f'freedom from afar . . .

They hold meetings, protest, bring
Ireland-n-Central America to my
attention in my mailbox . . . but

this Joe Strange, teaches a course
in how to speak English-n-act human, he
says to me th'world's become selfish.

Joe says that down in Central America, soldiers,
dictators, death squads; Joe said to me, Father,
I could do alot jest goin' with him onna

short trip with some help, let 'em
see all Americans aren't their
common man's enemy . . . Joe

said, Father, somethin'
like my goin' with him would be
somethin' with nuthin' visible

in it for me. 'Course we could git slabbed, I
think what I'm tryin' to tell you, Father,
is I think I see my life's need-n-I

put all this down f'you
now th'rest is for
old Boppledock.

III

    Here in green life old truck
    carrying American aid bounces
    Boppledock and Joe Strange like pancakes

    flip over up and down on their seats
    traveling mud ruts. It is like
    meadows of Custer . . .

    Boppledock Sixty-Six
    at least in real action,
    now in it, the

    bullets throw him out of truck and smack
    him on his back. Joe Strange behind
    steering wheel when the picture

    goes out of his eyes, looking
    for it through windshield. Bop aware
    that several are taking what is in truck

and vanishing like he wasn't lying
there. No one comes to fire
bullet into his head, these

are peasants, it is a shrug.
If he can manage to live
alright! . . .

IV

. . . In the tiny little bit of Ireland
my Grandfather, The O'Dock, ever saw
as a little child in dust's death

never did he see a black man. Come here to
America he and his mother hardly found
any blacks even on a clear blue lobster-water

country side street . . . People weren't
outside their ghettos mingling in among
the white Protestants, trying to

could cost you your life in clear blue
lobster-water country ignorance,
cruelty, bullying, forcing anyone

you found frightening to do vile things
in lobster frustration, always gettin'
up early cold-n-workin' wind cold

sea slappin' you like a snaked belt buckle
until your joints seized up before you
were even forty, there wasn't much in

your life, not even radio then, hardly any
blacks either in the clear blue lobster-
water country . . . "too cold f'em-n-they like

sugar-n-hot places!" Maybe one. One tall one,
maybe one lean one down at th'sardine factory, who know
why he comes s'far up north where th'green

in th'Pines is always blood deep
green-n-th'cold never really
goes away even onna bright hot

orange lobster stew day when
th'clouds in th'sky look like
butter in milk-n-all th'tourists

in their purple shorts-n-flappy hats are
thinkin' 'bout swimmin' mebbe drivin'
over t'Old Orchard where you could git in

by Googins' rocks-n-it's pretty warm but
always th'chill never leaves, why a black man
even thought he could escape whatever overwhelmin'

Harlem he run frum witha woman-n-two little-uns,
what'ud he think would be better here . . . mebbe
jest livin' in among faces of other colors . . .

. . . Now thet don' seem like thet 'ud be hit!
Whut could hit be!? One lean black at
th'sardine factory who stood out so

y'didn't have t'look very hard t'find where
he lived, collapsin' brick inside which
a couple a'wide-eyed innocent black faces and a

woman impassive lest an expression from her
git them killed or evicted-n-Colon Foocum he say
he ain'na gonna wuk with no . . . but Mr. Ross a'Ross Sardines
   say

yessir he gonna 'cause th'powerful young black
ten times th'wukker any one a you is—seems
this man wants his job t'feed his family, so,

Colon Foocum git th'boys-n-
they show this black some goo-ud lobster fun
yesindeedie! Ayuh I know hit! until it whispered

up-n-down th'wharfs you could play with this black.
Have you fun! . . . you could play with this un he
wants his job s'bad in rubber apron an' boots, in

th'rubber people who wuk with fish all th'time gettin'
hosed of fish scales wear-n- it was
whispered in snicker that he had a dong

on him he could git all th'way up a'elephant,
yesireebob! He'd show it t'you 'f you told him
he might not be needed no more at th'sardine

factory-n-some a'th'boys led by Colon Foocum'ud
git him out back-n-taken theirn out-a-make
him take his out-n-git on his

knees-n-put theirn in 'is mouth while
he jerkin' thet big thing a'hissen
like Colon tell him—then

they'd tell him they like th'dark meat of fish
out back a'th'sardine factory on th'rickety
little platform, hidden, with nuthin' but

lobsters t'see 'f they wanna-n-th'men
several who go t'church Sundays-n-always
turn out th'light never lettin' even their wives

ever see theirn, gathered roun' t'watch,
they wouldn't none a'them taken theirn out-n-have
Colon Foocum ever able t'say

they had theirn right out 'long withhissen-goo-ud
Christian hardwukkin' God-fishin' fellas from
th'isolation called futility . . . Colon he say

no furrener better think he cummin' inta th'clear
blue lobster-water country-n-take a payday
frum any real American like th'Foocums since

they took th'handcuffs offa Fester Foocum
inna earliest settlin', they only
so many fish-n-so many jobs . . . ayuh I know hit!

>   V

>   . . . No longer Ellis Island, my Father,
>   but on toothpicks with sails
>   sinking all the way from Cambodia

>   and in boats impossible to float
>   from Vietnam, the sea permits
>   them to beach on America . . .

> . . . Just last week these
> were eating field mice in their squeals
> for fresh warm life-sustaining
>
> live blood and protein . . . Now
> entering my America, my culture
> through Los Angeles, here,

Father, is where San Salvador is now
if San Salvador can get here! This rush
from death can suffocate

you and me become
Coca-Cola Home Fries soft
on the evening of the

Mushroom taking our last blinding
picture like Christ rising from the dead.
You have shown us how You did it, God, enough!

Father, to survive
we must hunger like these
rice-paddy skeletons

come now desiring
your lust, your
open door.

> . . . Lying here Boppledock sees
> Mrs. Bop in that flash we all
> suffer, flash of going down . . .

Once I would have caught your breath for you!
What lasts longer, the knotty thick tree
or fleeting wildflower that stirs

your blood but wilts? Come, lady,
let me stick my sword in you hard
and pulsing my life, whispering

I love you in your acorn hair still
fresh from country hay and lust. Soon
it could be you, my love, looking

a splashed pumpkin grin cut
that holds my heart. Oh I have looked
like death, lady, for a long time now

layers of age over youth, glass windows
over eyes desiring. We become good-looking
as we near permanence . . .

"There, easy now!"
He was hearing words,
Boppledock realized.

"You've got luck!" a grinning
accordion jello face
was moving the words

into Boppledock's hearing
like that wish we all have to
come back from our graves granted.

"Your pal, identification says
Joe Strange, looks like he's
looking at some centerfold."

"Joe's alright?" Boppledock
tried to move but seemed
held down though nothing held him.

"Easy—you're hit . . . no, your
Strange friend took it neat
right in the center of his forehead

but the strange thing is his look is
as if he got answers, it's fine
with him!" This accordion jello face

seemed surrounded by other men who looked
just like the men who shot him. "It's
tragic, Mr. Dock. We got here from

Headquarters Command in time to tell these
gentlemen that you're on their side.
They find it hard to know which

Americans are which."
—"That's th'world today" . . . Boppledock
dozed . . . Father, I tried

to be a part of it and almost got slabbed but
it's better to go home and sit on my stoop knowing
it's not th'barstool of a loser it's

my front porch
that I look my chances for, my
share of this earth, Father . . .

>. . . Bop suddenly was aware that
> everything was dead silence now
> here where he lay on a stretcher in

> Central America, turning his head he
> didn't turn it far . . . There, just on
> the rim of his left eye, directly into it

> as he turned his head was the hole
> of an automatic pointed right at him
> by one of the young guerrillas . . . it

> was like enemy were passing them close
> so near they dared not make sound and
> if Bop did, even accidentally, even if he

> couldn't control a sneeze, the way
> we can't sometimes, especially times that
> embarrass us, when somebody is speaking or

> a magician performing and our sneeze breaks
> everyone's concentration . . . but if Bop
> breathed, so much as shifted his

> uncomfortable position and anything
> happened, shooting started, they all
> had to run, the young guerrilla

> would black out Bop in orange forever . . .
>   he
> was without expression, his eyes cat's-
> eye marble, he and Bop waiting for danger
>   to go.

VI

An ale of sea filled Bop's head, now,
memory, like an overwhelming wave
large like a tongue, to smash a beach . . .

. . . Bop, facing, suddenly, lying here
in Central America . . . I had to run
outa th'clear blue lobster-water country where

th'deep soul heart of me is, rush outa there from
frightened people, savage in their frustration,
over me in deep depression kickin'

you quick outa th'way more than
ever takin' care a'you, a plate
of cold food, Franco-American Spaghetti

outa a can opened fast-n-thrown at you
with a snarl-n-you better not complain
or ask for seconds, or you'd go

right to bed without anything! Meanness
is from nothing you ever do
bringing you happiness . . .

. . . Th'sea never pays well, it makes you
into th'froth of its waves . . . Th'lobster ocean
is loud, you have to speak up, your

opportunity can be drowned. Jimmy Economo
yelled loud! He talked loud, you could hear
Jim Economo loud wherever he

was, in Luke's Coffee Pot next to
Chuck's Clothes, especially in his office.
You could hear Jim way out in th'middle

of th'street, you'd think folks wuz
deaf th'loud way Jim Economo said anything!
Jim, second-generation Greek in a

silent, quiet Protestant New England, become
a big lawyer, District Attorney, though
they always sent some climber from

th'Prosecutor's office over t'Augusta if
a case wuz anythin' goo-ud, worthwhile, a
murder a'suthin' like 'at, goo-ud-Jimmy

Economo'd never git them! They
coulda made him celebrated,
t'warn't no one gonna let a Greek

shoeshine boy have suthin' like 'at no sir rebob!
Jimmy Economo was a success in a trap. This was
Protestant clear blue-n-don' no one wanna forgit it.

VII

Lime City has become hamburger stands now
and unskilled crime committed
from despair's overwhelming fatigue,

ignorance's inability to do better, crimes
dangerous only by accident, you're liable
t'git hurt 'f you suddenly come upon

someone in th'process a'tryin' t'take
th'stereo outa y'car . . . th'old-timers
used t'gettin' by on nothin' yet

somehow with enough-n-retired,
can't explain it to themselves, what
are dreams 'f you can't afford 'em . . . still

the sea blood blue some days and
sharp in your nose, sea smell clear clean
with the death of the sardine on its breath

like the stench in the air in paper mill towns
mingled with lobster fresh salt sea air
smell of lobsters thrust up in their traps, seaweed

clinging like strangling podded ropes though
their own greed, as all ours,
predicts their end . . . and in

traps set down where they crawl with all their
tufted spindle legs, feelers on anything
to eat until it is us who will eat them.

In lobster towns the silence
of death as a business keeps faces'
lips tight without knowing why, maybe.

Maybe we don't know why! The sea is grim
when you reach in her until you have scooped her out,
taken all her lobster forever.

VIII

"We all tried to get Jim Economo to listen, to
hear us!" Attorney-at-law Young Billy Dock said
to his brother, Bop,

sitting at a hotel dining room table,
looking out on ocean, clear blue lobster-
water blue, blue-green, Sea Gull splashed

and lobsters, moving devouring garbage cans
of the sea, eating everything along
the shook seafloor . . . which

makes their sweet meat, death makes
food for life . . . Bop reminisced,
"Jimmy Economo shined shoes all his boyhood."

"Specifically, what are you saying!?" Young Billy
asked, thinly veiling exasperation . . .
. . . "Until," Bop finished,

"he almost developed a permanent subservient hump
from bending over shoes to snap a shine
on them, and he walked around spittoons

with an apron on with pockets to put nickels
in he collected from Pool players, dropping
nickels into the apron pockets along with

shoeshine money, finally he burst out
of it to law school . . ."
"We advised Jimmy that our considered opinion was

not to get Savas out of Augusta
State Hospital." Young Billy
started again . . . Bop interrupted, "Jimmy insisted?"

Young Billy picked up his drink and said,
"Wouldn't listen. You know how loud
Jim Economo can be!" . . . Bop, carefully,

"He was rising above th'pool tables . . ." Young Billy
looked at Bop as he might at a witness, or someone he was
certain was guilty, but, nevertheless, would represent . . .

"Well," Young Billy continued, "much against our
good counsel, Jim Economo brought his client, Savas,
here and took him into his office."

"Don't tell me," Bop blurted, "Jim got lobster-grabbed!"
"Yes," Young Billy looked momentarily amused, "that's
exactly it, all hell broke loose, as you

put it, lobster claw pinched good! When they got inside
Jimmy Economo's office and Jimmy had Savas sat down
to listen to his wisdom, Savas shot him five times."

IX

It was always vague exactly where
Paul Economo came from to the
clear blue lobster-water country . . . he

was a wonder! A wonder and a worker!
He started a shoeshine stand-n-added
a poolroom right across from Mae's Ice Cream

Parlor. Fishermen came in with
sea stink in their clothes, stomach-
wrenching smell of fish and relit cold cigars,

while Paul Economo, then
Paul Economo-n-his four boys,
walked around collecting nickels for pool games

and shined shoes. Big Billy, Smilin' Billy,
forbade Bop to ever go in there while
he'd stop outside, make a point

of stopping on Main Street, right out there publicly
on Main Street where word of who wuz speakin' t'who
spread up-n-down Main Street from one end t'other;

Big Smilin' Billy outside Paul Economo's
where he could be plainly seen talkin' to
Paul Economo, yesindeedie, ayuh, I know hit-n-Paul

Economo beaming, Big Billy smilin' that
Smilin' Billy smile a'hisen, chattin' affably
with Paul Economo beaming at talking with

one a'th'white chosen, who, while not Protestant but
Irish, even Catholic!—was quality worth talkin' to in
that New England town, telling everyone,

Big Billy telling everyone what a
hard worker and good man Paul Economo was but
forbidding Bop ever to go in Paul's, which in

Big Billy's I must be appeased imagination
never needed checking on all the years
Boppledock was in Paul's every day being

welcome for his nickels while looked at with
contempt as spoiled, no account . . . Young
Billy Dock wuz what any Pool shark-ud want

a boy a'his t'be like . . . one by one the sons
of Paul Economo left the Lime City where
old Paul had hoped they'd settle,

Ralph, to Rhode Island, nuthin' more-n-a truck driver,
Joe, to th'Merchant Marine, never wrote, Bobby, th'glamour boy
driftin' America a Golf bum . . . but Jimmy,

Jimmy to law school, Paul Economo's pride,
shot for trying to help
one of their own . . .

    . . . Bop told Young Billy he'd be right back,
    got up and walked out of Young Billy's
    sight for a few minutes, as if he

    was going to the men's room, making a
    phone call, suddenly sitting there had
    become overwhelming, he could see

    Jimmy Economo, a boy, times after school
    Bop'ud come into Paul's with snow, brush-

ing off
snowflakes, Jimmy smiling, proud, no

submission, in fact an arrogance in
the way he'd shine shoes, and he looked
like a wise owl coming from collecting

in the poolroom, like he saw his university,
his law school in the jingling change in
his pockets . . . Once, when the Athletic

Coach at Lime City High School was
threatened with losing his job, Peggy
Croft, of The Crofts, told Bop if he

and that Jimmy Economo didn't stay
out of it, stop going round getting
signed student petitions protesting

the Coach's dismissal, their names
would be mud in Lime City, but that
made Big Billy furious that even a Croft

would dare say to a Dock, now, these
days, that he couldn't stand up for
an Athletic Coach, Poetry'ud be

somethin' else, but anybody gifted at
teachin' how to round third-n-spike goo-ud
oughta be stood up for, so with

Big Billy approving, which delighted
Paul Economo, that a son of his was
exercising democracy with th'son of

a real American, Jim and Bop, Bop and
Jim, were close for a minute, exercising
principle and ethics, and saved th'Coach's

job, then fell apart back into
their positions, but Bop
never forgot the expression

of Greek democratic fierce
pride in Jimmy Economo's
look . . .

X

. . . Again now, Young Billy signaled
for another drink . . . "A couple of years ago,"
he began again, "This Greek like

Jim Economo's Greek . . ." Bop nodded,
"This Savas got angry at some lawyer
over around Bangor, kept insisting

the lawyer cheated him and he shot him."
"What they do?" Young Billy waved
to the waiter again . . . "They prosecuted . . . Open-

and-shut case! Any Prosecutor, ANY Prosecutor
would love it!!" Their drinks arrived . . . Outside
against the lobster sky, tired lobstermen

started in with the day's haul. The weather cold
clean sharp sea salt wind on the clear blue . . . Young
Billy commented, "He, Savas, got declared

insane."—Young Billy's features took on
a stern disapproval, as he
said, "He didn't wound that first lawyer badly."

"That . . . first lawyer!!?" Bop was taken aback!
Young Billy looked hard at Bop.
"Yep, that first lawyer! Well after about

eight months in Augusta State Hospital another
lawyer gets Savas a pass, how he did it or why,
don't ask me. He's out! He goes to see the

lawyer who just loosed him back among us after
nearly a year and he shoots him too!" Bop
intentionally looked aghast, allowing

Young Billy to have his I must be appeased
attention so he'd continue, not frown, not
recede within himself in the sulk of drinking

convinced Bop wasn't listening to his show, his
obviously insightful description, he imagined.
—"Well, our Jim Economo, second-generation

Greek from Poolroom to D.A. to
Private Practice, good-hearted Jim Economo wasn't
going to have it said of him in the

Lime City he grew up in of the
clear blue lobster-water country, that a
countryman of his could have trouble and

be alone, no sir! no sir rebob! Jim
Economo, all Paul Economo has left except
his girls, his daughters." Young Billy stopped,

as if he had finished a summation . . . Yeah, his
girls, Bop realized, Paul Economo's got girls but
he wouldn't think girls matter! Bop said now,

"Jim Economo stepped up out of shoeshining
to walk with Protestants and eat th'same
lobster they do . . ." Bop shook his head and said, "Jim

jest couldn't resist tryin' to shove
a little wiseass at whispering Protestants
who would keep him stooped shining shoes his

whole life if they could . . . if it wasn't
for his immigrant father, a wonder,
and for his own hard hard work in law school, to give

the clear blue lobster-water country Protestants a
message, loud, that we Greeks are together!"
"Guess what!?" Young Billy said, "He decided to

represent Savas . . . worse." Bop waited.
Young Billy went on, "The first
thing he did was to tell this Savas, his

client, that he'll get him out of the
State hospital." . . . "I can't believe this!" Bop
squirmed around in his chair. Lips pursed,

Young Billy said, "Those of us who practice
law pointed out to Jim Economo that
Savas's aim was getting better, but you

couldn't get Jim to listen. Savas was his client
and, as important, unable to speak good English and
nobody was going to keep a Jimmy Economo

client locked up awaiting proceedings."
"How," asked Bop, shaking his head . . . "How,
under any stretch of anybody's imagination,

did Savas become bailable!" "Who knows!?"
Young Billy mused and grinned as if
privately enjoying lawyer ability . . . "That's

what lawyers are around for, to do the
impossible!" Young Billy sucked his glass.
The smooth hoochino was beginning

to make him look preserved. "I guess
when he got to the point where psychiatrists
thought him well enough to issue a pass so he

could confer with the second lawyer about
shooting and wounding the first lawyer, I
guess that somehow, technically, even though he

shot his second lawyer, too, and was now answerable
for two shootings, I guess, somehow, being able to
get a pass got him to some weird status where

Jim Economo could get him out on bail, if he
could post it." "Humanity backfired on Jim," Bop
commented. Young Billy looked at Bop waiting . . .

"Trying to be compassionate," Bop finished, "to
raise another immigrant to the treatment a white
Protestant would expect, got Jim Economo shot."

They could see lobstermen
far away now toward their
beaches, tired, the death of the day

ready to be sorted on rough piers,
wharves that looked rickety in tar gravel
and the lobster gone out of the Penobscot forever.

Bop said, "Think, Young Billy . . . all Jimmy
Economo's hard hard work, everything went
out the bullet holes in him." "No, he's

recovering," Young Billy stated. They both would
leave the Lime City Hotel dining room now and
outside on the sidewalk, part, Young Billy fast.

Holding the hotel door open for them, Bop mused,
"Somehow, I don't think anybody could be
th'same after somebody shot you." . . . Walking by

himself up Main Street past Paul Economo's
Pool Parlor, shoeshine business, Bop tried
to fantasize his Father, to see Big Billy,

Smilin' Billy standing, talking there . . . right
there!! . . . with Paul Economo . . . instead Jimmy
Economo filled his mind, he could hear the shots.

. . . The first bullet, Jim's arms become like
snapped twigs that, muscled, rippled snapping
shines on shoes . . . and bullet two took his

body's generated strength to lift him above it all.
Shot three canned his ambition in his wounds, and
after shot four, all his heart's lust

out the sieve of him . . . the fifth bullet
made certain he must always admit a
companion to his privacy . . .

XI

My Grandfather, Michael The O'Dock,
from County Clare, Ireland,
ordered a house to be built of granite

in Portland, Maine, of the clear blue
lobster-water country. It is war awful
to have your old home bombed to a wall

staggering in its sweat, a sliver of ghosts,
but as bad to have the house your Grandfather
ordered built still there but lived in by

strangers because in America whole families
made believe they were who they weren't, the
immigrant foolishly proud to brag

that no child of his would ever
have to do what he had to do, have to know
what one who is transplanted must survive,

suffer, in order to get a house
and education for his children in the
colleges; but no instinct who they

really were: nobodies because they
had no real money under them always
in eviction's shadow . . . and hidden

in among them, frantic masses
coming to America, potential
assassins with no apparent grudge.

XII

. . . Now breezes on Bop's face, like
licking tongues, lying here
on a stretcher, the inside head's

razor-slicing memory—Mrs. Bop and
Lollibop came with me t'New York
as I left f'here . . .

They were suddenly frantic at
m'sudden goin' as underneath all
th'bitchin' was love . . . They were

scared, intuition feared we all
would never see each other again . . .
. . . M'sudden goin', comin' here

to my life, at last participatin',
at last inna world I sidestepped
swillin' ale-n-excuses . . . arrivin'

in New York . . . "Wanna cab," drenching
downpour, grab your suitcases; in
The Drake lobby, hidden in the cubicle

where you buy newspapers, Bop
suddenly saw Lollibop being cruised
by a smooth Dutch young man and when

she smiled her baby look suddenly
peeked through her 28-year-
old flush of happy youth being
   approached,

and they were walking over to the
lobby bar opposite the elevators as
Bop crossed the lobby and went up to be
   with

Mrs. Bop who had made his whole life
   valuable,
even when sunk in drink he could not but
fail her and now going off to Central

America on her, in order to be
part of life he had been so broken in
childhood as to be unable to get into

anything, he was now, again, abandoning
her . . . What is it that makes us
think we'll find everything

anywhere else than where
it's always been, in the arms of our love
and our children, but we do! We always

do it, run to look where nothing is, what
is it in us that breaks the hearts
of the only people who love us? Robbed
   of

our mother's cradling, a never-filled
loss, and we cannot seem to stop ourselves
from abandoning what we have! Loved
   ones, life

with them, their love of us, yet we seek
   as if
we feel we are violated out of our share
of . . . What!!?, while we give

everyone else smiles, our charm acting
as we think we are expected
to with everyone who doesn't matter . . .
  Just

. . . then . . . now lying here on
Central American ground, hurt, the face
  of
Smilin' Billy, of Big Billy, filled Bop's

head and the old ache back, spraining his
nerves so they were like a thousand ants
having their feast of him . . . Fa-ther . . .
  in

Bop's . . . thoughts—Fa-ther, this fat little
gray man with th'potbelly snout . . . is . . .
Lahty! . . . FATHER, it's Lahty! NOW,
  Father

. . . tell me that you love me . . . now . . .
. . . Pressure like fingers reaching for
him slipping, Bop seeming to slip out of

the fingers' grasp of something, as if
he was something becoming slippery to
something trying to take hold of him . . .
  then

as suddenly he felt alright, the
frightening was gone . . . Bop raised
himself up a bit now, all around

him the guerrillas were coming and going,
  it
seemed aimlessly, they didn't seem
to really be going anywhere, yet,

Bop realized they knew what
they were about . . . They're
tryin' t'do here what

we come to America t'do, Bop
fumbled with it . . . like
. . . m'Grandfather, like

Michael The O'Dock, my Grandfather
. . . rushing
to America with his hand clutched
in his mother's . . .

XIII

All Michael The O'Dock did in America
is almost vanished; there are not
even Headstones with the names

of his children on them in the
South Portland, Maine, graveyard, and not one of them
would have a plot to lie in either if Michael

The O'Dock hadn't himself bought enough land
to hold eleven of his thirteen children and
his mother and his wife and himself forever in

South Portland, Maine, of the clear blue lobster-
water country. None of my Grandfather Michael
The O'Dock's daughters have headstones with

their names on them over their graves.
It is as if they were all stillborn but
they weren't and lived to be old.

XIV

Accordion jello face came over
and got down on his haunches
by Boppledock.

"How you feeling?" his leathered
face was like it had been slashed deep
by knuckles of razors but it hadn't,

years of serving under the sun
and weather made the face give
where it had to, lines allowing

the skin to stay in one piece.
"I don' know how I feel!" Bop replied
hardly sorry at his irritability . . .

"Can I get you something we got?"
"No thanks." Bop suddenly looked at him—
"You're not Spanish?" "No I'm

part of the U.S. Army that's here
jes' visitin'." He grinned. "I came
here to look," Bop said, "to see

if I could help little people get
to vote, pick their system." Accordion
jello face tried to hide his

opinion of that but couldn't mask
his look. Bop asked, "Do you think we
ought to come here for Dictators?"

Accordion jello face put his palms up.
"I'm jes' a soldier, if I live through it,
jes' live through this right here, I get

out! Master Sergeant Alfred Kelly is
out, through!!" Bop looked up at him so
hard he felt like he'd wrenched his

neck. "Kelly!?" "That's th'name!"
. . . Bop scowled . . . "There's always so
many Kellys, never th'right one!" Bop

let himself down to lie flatter . . . "You
been lookin' for somebody named Kelly,
I'll
ask around, I m'se'f didn't know

they wuz another Kelly out here with us . . .
What's th'Kelly you want's first name?"
"I never knew" Bop drifted . . . Master

Sergeant Alfred Kelly stood up, in the
uncertain way of the confused who

can't be sure just what you're saying to
them, he shrugged, shot a wave of his hand
   at
Bop and walked off . . . Just then home

        overwhelmed Bop's thoughts . . . the waste
          of
lobster until they'll all be gone. Eaten by
farmers come in from their

planting, themselves grown a part
of their crops; lobstermen bent at
their hauling dead weight from deep

ocean, crustacean ignorant
of their scavenging: lobster
ravished off their rocks to

feed selfishness not necessity, and
tourists eating them to feel they're
getting something special for all the

hours of their drudgery, yet
unconsciously guilty, aware you don't
just go get lobster like you

pick an apple off a tree because
like cow udders bursting unmilked
you either pick the apple or

the tree throws it to earth for the pigs
or to rot, but lobsters would
continue living and crawling,

clearing the salt green sea
of its refuse if we didn't
drop traps for them.

      XV

Father we'll
meet again.

You can tell me you love me then.

Mother, you have always been lost to me.
I hope there comes a time
when the game's over

and I can see you . . . life ends and you
become mine forever in among
you and those you always wished

to be with forever, your dead,
as you and Father are my never
forgotten dead, as my wife and I

will be our daughter's dead. Do
the dead all erase death
eternally together? What keeps

us without struggle and disappointment
if the dead do not erase death?
Now I'd like, Mother, to believe

the stupid struggle life is ends
and you become mine forever
in among you and those you always wished

to be with forever, your dead, as you
and Father are my never-forgotten dead . . . as
my wife and I will be our daughter's

dead . . . Do the dead all erase death? What
keeps us in some place called Heaven without
struggle and disappointment? . . . What do we do when

our excuses and blame are used up, gone, and there
we all are with each other . . .? Mother, would
it be better if we never met?

Is that what happens, yearning is only a device
to get us through this earth living until
we have earned whatever complicated

eternity is ours for our evil or our goodness but in it
there are no reunions, our life was our life
and while we are what we call alive

on this earth, we miss those who impregnated
and carried us—in our fright
of the unknown and our ignorance . . . Mother, Father,

I hope you are there when the Moon dips low
and I catch my ride . . . when the sweet scent
of Maine is just caught where my breath ends.

XVI

Baptized without choice when I was hardly born,
Confirmed into a religion I did not choose,
I was to break in terror of You and eternal damnation,

a toddler genuflecting and blessing myself or else!
"God will strike you dead if you do this!"
"God will strike you dead if you do that!" screeched

Big Billy who was afraid of God. So terrified
of You God, he was on his knees
when he needed to be up on his feet . . . I've

broken your most serious commandments, the ones
you never get to "see You" if you
do them; I've done that thing I

was taught I'd burn in Hell forever
if I did it, never ever see Your
face! . . . Let me say I'll

take whatever I've coming. I have faith
in You that Dante's Hell is Dante's need,
imagined pain becomes real pain in human need to

know a feeling that could get worse, and
makes possible reverent, fervent worship
of incomprehensible religion; people

close their eyes, moan and rock
thinking everyone knows what they're doing,
but most of all God knows so they'll

be saved in some Saturday afternoon
matinee Heaven with Lon McCallister and
June Haver in a lovely meadow green,

sunshine happy forever, forgetting that
here on earth we leave our paradisiacal
vacations worn out, tired of the beach,

weary of our last resort, back to rush and struggle,
but purity of motive is harder to achieve
than the hardest betrayal. Greed and neon

flickering death, anything to "get the order"—
Like Roman Church allowing Bop's friend Buffer Rose to
get his booze dollars hustlin' *La Catolica*

door to door flashing some imprimatur,
kept inside plastic against rain, that
has a picture of some Bishop in vestments

in the middle of the most important part of
The Mass, like giving Communion, a sight
certain to intimidate; Buffer Rose

with this imprimatur, like identification from God
Himself, sellin' magazine subscriptions by
terrifying poor guilty who do not dare

close their doors, once Buffer calls out,
knuckles pounding their locked doors,
"Th'church!" "Fa-ther sent me!"

"Saint Anthony, ma'm" . . . "San Antonio, Mamma!"
. . . and before they can open their mouths—"Who you
wanna Mass said for, y'Father, y'Mother . . .? It's

only Five ($5.00) for two years," Buffer
writin' th'order already as he speaks;
these people won't turn him away,

thinking of themselves, hoping
someone on earth will help pray them
finally into Heaven when they're not

on earth anymore where you can always
fall down on your knees and atone,
after they can't . . . half of each $5.00 order

is Buffer's, $1.25 to some vague Seminary
he uses in his pitch, "for poor boys who
wanna study for th'Priesthood"

he tells everyone; the Seminary prob'ly exists
and gets a trickle of quarters, just
barely keeping this legal . . . or the $1.25 each

order goes directly to Archdiocese, and $1.25
each order to shrewd hustler businessman,
Baldy Knox, who thought this up, said

to Father, "Can't harm anyone, gettin' a good
religious magazine-n-you will say th'Masses-n-
it'll get you cash from people who

don't come to Mass, so you'll never get their coin
in your collection basket" . . . Who . . . can prove it!?
Names, names, names of people's loved ones for whom

they've accepted another magazine into their house
in the resignation that at least Masses
are being said for someone they loved

to help them get into Heaven. Names
scribbled often quick by Buffer, maybe
not even written clearly if he's

movin' smooth, makin' sales-n-tryin'
t'hit as many doors as he can
before it rains or somebody calls th'Police . . . the

names handed to his sales crew chief, somebody
called Joe Egan or Mafia-soft low-key Vinnie Cura;

th'names of everyone who is to have
a Mass said for them, religiously
taken into Baldy Knox's office-n-Baldy Knox

lickin' his thumb thumbin' th'money . . .
Vinnie Cura explained to Buffer,
calmly, the day he joined them . . .

"We're doing them all such a
wonderful favor. They're guilty
poor people who don't have the

money to keep going out visiting
graveyards and it embarrasses them
to go to church Sundays with no

money to give, so, here we'll
take only $3.00 or $5.00 and
we make out, Baldy Knox makes out,

and they make out, know what I mean?
We tell them a Mass will be said for
those they can't afford, for their

Five dollars . . . They can afford it!"
Buffer, indignant, "Th'church, th'Seminary
gets money, too . . . n-th'Masses do

get said!!?" Vinnie Cura hissed,
"Of course they do," almost inaudibly . . . but
it bothered Buffer, who, like Bop,

had a lawyer brother, Atlee Rose,
staunch Catholic, never missed Mass,
went to Confession, Communion, prided himself

as head of claims for an insurance company, in
settling claims like where a woman had
lost both legs and sued for millions,

for Five Thousand out of court. She
couldn't wait, needed money, was
hungering for dollars; yet Atlee Rose

was calling Buffer a bilker of old ladies
for selling this *La Catolica* . . . It bothered
Buffer, Atlee must be right, must have

somethin' to do with education making what
Atlee Rose did to little people alright, but
Buffer wrong; f'example, who knows if

these names are ever given to a Priest to
say Masses, or if they are, if they're all then
not just dumped in a pile and one

Mass said, which in the goodness
and greatness of dear God is
supposed to be good enough? Who

would question that God didn't
see y'Father, y'Mother among a million
names hastily written by a

salesman moving fast while th'sun's shinin'? . . . and
. . . in America of The O'Dock from
County Clare, Ireland, Irish

committing sin certain to guarantee
your waiting a long time, if ever
you could get into Heaven out of

Purgatory or Limbo . . . brother
betraying brother for his own fresh start,
using education your own brother came to

America with his hand clutched in your mother's
and sweat to get you, to cheat him . . .
It was hunger that drove us out of Ireland,

still we could not see that when it came to it,
the church heavy on us had no miracle,
could not make potatoes where none

would grow anymore . . . Could not bless us luck
in strange savage lands, even if we
brought God along in our imagining . . .

XVII

My Grandfather, The O'Dock from
County Clare, Ireland, ordered a house
to be built of granite in Portland, Maine,

city of sardine stink and Burnham & Morrill
baked beans, oh it was elegant
for a self-made man to have his success

in America, what he accomplished from the
emigration from County Clare, Ireland, gone
forever from County Clare of his heart,

Clare of the sea and potato scabs, shadow
Ireland, land of starving and sure death if
you stayed. Jesus wouldn't make potatoes grow

f'all y'genuflectin' to Him and moanin' to
keep His broken faithful home
in His goodness and wisdom knowin'

what's best. He dispossessed the Irish.
. . . no one special because they're
Catholic or Protestant or anything a'tall a'tall.

XVIII

. . . My Grandfather, Michael The O'Dock,
ordered a house to be built of granite
in America, a good Irishman

who with his hand clutched in his mother's
came to this country on his childish guts
and staggered under luggage still a boy

as a baggage Porter in Portland, Maine,
railroad station until his mother, saving,
got enough for a grocery store, then five

and sending the money home to Ireland, educating
one brother a doctor, the other a lawyer and
bringing them over to America. My Grandfather,

The O'Dock, left a granite house behind him in
Portland, Maine, of the clear blue lobster-
water country, not gone to the grave with him

but still standing for me to almost come apart
looking at it because I can't go in it anymore . . . no.
We were Irish Catholic broken unable to

motivate to earn until too late to keep
my Grandfather's house! A house filled with great
frustration, my only brother Young Billy had to break

with me forever and that house and those people,
my aunts, the daughters of Michael The O'Dock
embalmed alive in the Irish religion, frightened,

terrorized tip your forelock Irish while saying
they weren't, insisting they weren't!, trembling in
gratitude for school teaching jobs in among

the Protestants of New England . . . wishing
to be thought Irish but a picture of Queen Victoria
in many Irish-American bathrooms, not ours, we

were green, aunts living out their whole
unmarried lives in the house their father
The O'Dock built for them, never remembering

a kind word from "Himself" or any gesture that
he loved them. They were the duty his dong
fulfilled for the church more than they ever

were his children in the house he ordered built
of granite four stories high if you counted the
dining room and kitchen sunk where

a cellar should be; grand staircases up from each
end of the hall but only the one in the back hall
going downstairs . . . then both winding staircases,

winding circular up and around like
a cardinal's capa magna unfolding up two floors to where
what would be anyone else's attic had three bedrooms

one of them with a skylight window we used to call "Tip Top,"
it was a grand house built for a wife and thirteen
children only the last a boy, Big Billy,

right across the street from Saint Dominic's
Roman Catholic Church in Portland, Maine,
of the clear blue lobster-water country . . . My

Grandfather's lawyer brother victim of what
seems to be a particular Irish disease, dark terrible
treachery; to the British against their own and

especially in families seeming to resent
another's success or owing them. My Grandfather
Michael The O'Dock's own brother for whom he

half-killed himself as a little boy to
work to earn enough money to buy a grocery store
for them all in America and send the money home so

his brothers could get off the boat educated men, his
lawyer brother cheated him and their mother so that
all my boyhood in Portland, Maine, of the clear blue

lobster-water country, there were "us" the State Street
O'Docks and across the city where my Grandfather
and his mother began in Portland, Maine, the Munjoy Hill

O'Docks never speaking, all my boyhood . . . I was
on strict orders never to ever say even "hello"
to a Munjoy Hill O'Dock . . . The Irish do each other

more harm than anyone could think up
to do to them, there's a savage self-destructiveness
in us, we want death . . . want to reminisce

longingly about what could have been . . . My Grandfather
The O'Dock ordered a house to be built of granite
in Portland, Maine, of the clear blue lobster-water country

O'Dock emblazoned into the front door
on a thick bronze nameplate of the house my
Grandfather Michael The O'Dock built and

on the edge of the curb of the sidewalk in
front of the house, a big granite stone to step
out onto from horse-drawn carriages and

later, cars. Sometimes through the years
I drive all the way to Portland, Maine, from
wherever I am and sit in my car in

front of bleak redbrick Saint Dominic's,
furious in the stench of incense, across
the street from the house my Grandfather built

for us all, but times change and money's value.
We O'Docks though proud were dumb to the
real world, frightened by the Irish screaming faith,

beaten into us, eliminating us as competition.
We were submissives though it is a
treacherous mean low thing to say about your own.

My Grandfather's only son Big Billy spent his
life fantasizing himself as everything he wasn't
and would like to have been—a "Broadway
Dapper Dandy," "Fred Astaire," yet he wasn't ignorant.

The church and a spoiled bringing-up had him on
his knees. He was an educated man who
needed approval, to get back for what he suspected

he could never dare to put his finger on—had been
robbed from him, instilled with guilts, never
daring to make a move without getting down on his knees

and blessing himself and reciting endless
words called prayers in fear if he didn't
"God" would "strike him dead" . . . an educated man

who studied kitchen-Greek under John Alden, yes,
a descendant of who you think and liked to believe
he could kitchen-Greek with shoeshine parlor Greeks who,

in the problem of social climbing from one position to
another, were tickled, flattered that a man of the
fair-colored skin of the ruling Wasp with blue eyes, too, would

"tryna garble" whatever it was he tried to garble
with them from his Greek studies. They were all really
hustling together in this new land of opportunity

where money expresses how royal you are . . . Big Billy
used to be so frustrated, held back, restrained from
bursting forth, the real Big Billy! by two

children left him by a dead mother . . . Big Billy
used to scream, "God will strike you dead!"
to us, but he had a style and a smile for every adult.
He was afraid of grown-ups, only tough with weak

and helpless children, or people who worked for him . . . he
forgot children grow up and remember . . . Then he'd
"feel bad." Big Billy would feel bad

and meet you after school go buy you an ice cream
sundae which better make it alright! better
make everything alright! His seething fury threat

waited for you not to accept
an ice cream all right! But he was a
good man according to his lights. He needed

the Irish church permission but he was a
good man, the best of the broken Irish
descended from a man of futile courage

who stumbled here to America, his hand clutched
in his mother's from God's empty potato fields
and said goodbye forever to County Clare . . . Clare

of wild violet Irish Atlantic like the
clear blue lobster-water country, fresh in salt,
the wind screaming your heart's lust joy in its whistle

and down deep the lobsters crawling oblivious as
all God's good creatures about their murders as if
no one knows and they are ordained for it, so,

when we sink our traps, it is our killing . . . it was
only little children Big Billy raged at, raged his
own bitter disappointments on, biting

a handkerchief and screaming until
his face burst bloodred frothing spittle
rolling down his chin because he couldn't

muster himself for himself, and after all,
children always have been perfect victims, like
cats, small, not able to fight back against

"God will strike you dead" and "I must be appeased!"
Children "t'be seen-n-not heard-n-y'didn't
have a right to an opinion until y'30!"

XIX

Perhaps Big Billy secretly knew underneath his terror
that God wouldn't really strike you dead for
thinking for yourself, but too late that "God"

wouldn't "strike you dead" for being open-minded
and living this life He put you in trying
to imagine how to step on the Moon . . . Big Billy

somehow had been cheated, he sensed, but he couldn't
touch exactly what had been done to him and by whom,
certainly not by his lovely adoring wonderful mother,

not by The O'Dock, that he could see! Th-at he could see!!
Frothing red-faced in his spittle screech, his rage caught
in his handkerchief biting for the life robbed from him, he

could have been Damon Runyon!! . . . if he hadn't been made
to feel he better get right down on his knees praying
and asking God forgiveness, not out there, out competing,

out fighting for a piece of Protestantland . . . so, frustrated,
worse, not ever knowing why he was so angry he forced
his own children to loathe him for his screech

in sardine stench, all the petals
of wildflowers flew off their
stems in his bellow . . .

XX

. . . Oh and many an Irish immigrant youth
cursed by Saint Patrick myth and
stupidity, foolish pride bragging how

they were able to succeed enough to spare
their children what they had to do, and in
doing this, making many an Irish-American youth

as crippled as he is back home in
the rough green Irish Sea country but in
Ireland it's more from sheer futility

at lack of any opportunity to use your
talent through judgmental suppression into
the child in America where the Irish

fled to prosper from black potato core
the children of the immigrant's children
unable to speak for themselves, asking others

in the Protestant competition to put in
a good word for them while cold rain slammed
the window of warm house inside which

they were comfy cuddled right out of their lives in
Mother's cold next-day meat pies never getting
started, not able to go out and make themselves

stand up on their own two feet and open their mouths
and come right out and ask, ask! . . . even for
a sewer job . . . so ended American promise

in Michael The O'Dock . . . so ended the chance taking, the
beautiful riskers that are the greatness of a country,
ended the functioning that must come from

inside us in each and every one of us, promise
gone as much to the bottle here in America
as any Irish farmer with Ireland,

green Ireland, violent Ireland grape in its yearning,
Ireland always green in his eyes but alcohol
his early death with all the old boys crying

for The O'Dock who sailed away, his hand clutched
in his mother's forever from Ireland, Eire
of my soul my flesh wanders the earth . . .

XXI

Oh, my Grandfather The O'Dock ordered a house
to be built of granite right across the street from
God's house, Saint Dominic's Church in Portland,

Maine, of the clear blue lobster-water country. Truly
this granite house was Irish success in America.
But after the last daughter of Michael The O'Dock, my

Grandfather, died at 91 the house was sold, the
house that Michael The O'Dock came over to
America, as a little boy with his hand clutched

in his mother's, to rush from and survive
potato famine and earn enough to bring his
two brothers over just as soon as they could; all

the life's work, sweat of The O'Dock was just sold!
I, Bop, was unable to keep it . . . (didn't have any money)
(smell your own orifices) the house had no money

to keep itself. We were all poor from beating
our breasts in Mea Culpa instead of going out
into American opportunity with our lies and kiting checks

anything to keep our Grandfather's house. Anything!
We went our separate ways, Young Billy
so glad to escape me, to get away from the

stifling death in my aunt's and the suspicion
that all Bop, me, Bop wanted was to steal
money out of his wallet while he lay asleep in bed

in our Grandfather's granite house . . .
. . . He once told me he was watching me like a mouse,
meaning it too, he wasn't free of that house, those people,

Big Billy . . . and I had to rush away too, so looked like
a young bum running who would need support and Young Billy
wasn't going to give me any, I was on my own!

We are a damned breed, the Irish. Young Billy gave
his whole identity to Big Billy just to try
to have his love . . .

destruction of ourselves by ourselves
until we are all forgotten
dead among the dead . . .

XXII

. . . Throughout my manhood, throughout the
years, I often drive all the way back to
Portland, Maine, and sit in my car across

the street from the house I spent half my
boyhood in, I often go just to sit across the
street in my car to at least see the house my

Grandfather, Michael The O'Dock, built after coming
all the way from County Clare, Ireland, with
nothing a'tall. There were statements

in Help Wanted "No Irish need apply"
for the idea of America sold to the lowest
common man was that we would all be able to

worship God any way we wanted and beJesus-
screeching Irish Priests or Roman Catholic
worshipers were suspect of planning to

take over United States Constitution
just as soon as they could get enough
brush and firewood to start burning

people alive again who wouldn't take
the Wafer and the Mea Culpa . . . Often I
sit in my car in front of Saint Dominic's

Roman Catholic Church in Portland, Maine, of the
clear blue lobster-water country knowing someone
else has my home, but does not realize it, good

people, I'm sure, who must sense
a broken heart sitting across the street
in a car still in the scent of incense, but

they never open the door
or peer out so I sit
until I cannot.

XXIII

Here living in among other
immigrants of Protestant New England,
it was better to clip and harden your name

to make it easy for other people who,
after all, would be your customers as well as
neighbors, people who weren't Irish to say

your name easily, not be annoyed and go buy
bread and milk some place easy to say the
owner's name, so my Grandfather dropped the O

and became bluntly Mike Dock easy to
say, to hear, to deal with, not
aggravating, not anybody thinking

you were putting on airs in this
new country using some
fancy-sounding name like

"O'Dock" which was your name, but
not here, not in the Protestant
New England clear blue

lobster-water country, not here where
you've come just to eat, to stay alive
away from where potatoes wouldn't grow

where potatoes wouldn't
grow even if Jesus
asked them to Himself.

XXIV

In the old country, the Irish
would put on the headstones of
the graves left forever, the names

of Michael The O'Dock and his mother's
and his brothers' names on their
nearest relatives' gravestones, their

names and the dates they died
in America . . . and in America too
O'Dock went on my Grandfather's

own gravestone, but none of his children
even had identity enough in their
own minds to insist on their

names on headstones, there
are no names on the graves or
even stones over the graves of Michael

The O'Dock's children in America,
almost as if each and every one of them
felt he had never really wanted them.

His dong worked for the church
so he'd done his duty and could go
to Heaven, rather than wanting his

own children, no, they have no gravestones
but lie under the earth purchased for
them by their father doing what he

felt he had to do like wiping his ass
to be in good with Jesus, ravaging
his wife for a son until he got one

again and again, furiously, frantically
dong rape of the
mother of his twelve girls, girls don't count!

He wept, it was a family story that
he sat down on the steps of his granite house
and cried when he got the news that

after twelve girls he had Big Billy.
His girls now lie in the land he bought them
in the earth papa provided for them, as if

they never felt they had a right to purchase
their own forever place, as if they never felt
they had a right to put a stone

over themselves with their individual
names on it—No one can find them
and few are looking for them or ever will

or will ever visit them, even on Memorial Day.
They lived and died as if they'd never been
in America—in the clear blue lobster-water country

and the very name O'Dock, "Dock" lost vanishing
on His, The O'Dock's gravestone but what
planned revenge on him by his own girls, they

would never buy their own graves, their own earth
but lie in what he bought them with no
headstones over themselves, since he had never

wanted them or even picked them up when
they were little, to sit on his knee and be told
he loved them by him, so, after a lifetime of

consciously forever smelling their own orifices,
themselves as foul unwanted, they vanished forever
without a trace except in city and state and church

records in the clear blue lobster-water country
and the very name O'Dock lost—on Michael
The O'Dock's gravestone, but abbreviated in

his daily doings to make it easier to do business.
Yes, the name "O'Dock" is on Big Billy's gravestone,
Yes, it will be on Young Billy's and on mine too.

But the absence of it and the lack of gravestones for
any of Michael The O'Dock's daughters is that final **unseen**
unimagined failure that can come to us

who work so hard but inside ourselves, not
ever letting anyone we love know
we love them; it would bewilder us

that they would think we didn't, our
frustrated rage at being trapped by our income
let loose in silent resentment that is loud

in our house, misinterpreted,
our children thought we didn't want them . . .
while you yell that no man will ever

make you tip your forelock but doing it while
you're saying you're not and then feeling terrible
taking it out on your own children, so your soul

purpose is gone in the new land too . . . robbed
of our individuality by never hearing or
feeling our Father ever loved us, by the

browbeating tip-your-forelock
Roman Church, tricked out of life on
this earth for the next . . . "Dock" into the front door

of his granite house oh, it was
quite elegant for a self-made man to have!
From Ireland to America! Right across

the street from his parish
church, gone from the Docks in
less than sixty years . . .

XXV

. . . Father, it is night . . . see the
clear silk black death hovering to
enfold me . . . But I am not quite ready.

No one is ever going to be ready, we love to
think of an eternity in which we are finally happy
and it is always assumed that of course we'd

want to be with Mom and Dad and all our relatives
and old friends, when, perhaps, eternal
happiness is really oblivion, solitude in which

to contemplate and finally the answer as to the
"reason for everything," life, death, murder,
sorrow, torture, pain, why what was . . .

Father I'd
like to be the Apple Cheek kid
whose picture you

carried in your wallet
    once more
  oh, Father, once more!

      I
love you still . . . I remember
the smell of the sweat of you

in the old shirt you always left
on a hanger with a pair
of knickers, old clothes

to put on when you came to
the cottage in Old Orchard Beach, Maine,
of the clear blue lobster-water country.

I'd hug it to my nose in my loneliness
left at the beach where you thought a little boy
would want to be—but I wanted to be with you.

—but I was the kid who
reminded you too much of Mother . . . your
sister, my aunt, one of Michael The O'Dock's daughters

would say to me, when she noticed my need for you,
Father . . . how I mustn't mind if it seemed
you couldn't ever look straight at me much, I

reminded you so much of Mother that my aunt, your sister,
one of Michael The O'Dock's girls, said to me was why, I
looked so much like my mother you couldn't bear it; just

what was I supposed to do about it, vanish!? How should I
feel being told that I looked like the mother who had
to go somewhere and you could hardly stand looking

at me, I reminded you of her so much, when that
wasn't it!? You know and I know, from the times I've
wished I zipped up, Father, it could be every time

you saw me, had to look at me, knowing your Jesus-knit-browed
    Jesus
was probably gonna burn you in Hellfire forever and forever,
and, see how clever He is, part of your punishment right here

on earth before you get to leave to burn forever is having
to look at me, at what you did for which
God-ud strike you dead, it was never that

you were gonna go whether you were Arab,
Protestant, Jewish, no, it was me, me that
created your Hell, you did it but I was it . . .

We have killed our own seed in its ground.
But I slipped out in time, Mother,
I myself escaped.

XXVI

Big Billy lies buried in Thomaston, Maine, of
the clear blue lobster-water country, under a
headstone he bought economically. Already

the tombstone in just brief years since
Big Billy fell and hit that great bald head
to death on garage oil-stained concrete,

the tombstone is falling over with both Big Billy's
name and our mother's, names deeply embedded
as if once the stone was soft and their

names deep cut-in like by a cookie design, their
carved names are now filled with fungus green
although Big Billy dutifully paid for "Perpetual Care";

he's hardly in the ground and all meaning of him's
going, of his famous rages and Mea Culpa . . .
But in American Depression in which one was lucky

to have a plate of beans, especially with
fat slipping in among them, you
bought the surest thing you could so you'd

have it! The Economy Headstone even if
it did mean having your name and birth
date carved on it with the date of your own

death blank for you to have to see as the
weary years went by as you visited with
your two boys Bop and Young Bily the place

you told them, when you went there on her
birth date and your Wedding anniversary,
was where Mamma was but it was confusing and

you didn't dare ever ask, for fear Big Billy's
face would suddenly fill as if he was going
to blow a horn and turn beet red

before from deep within
him rage burst forth
an "I must be appeased!"

. . . Wasn't Mamma away taking care of a
little boy who needed her more than they did?
How come!? How come then we come to this place

a graveyard every time it's her birth date
or the two of you's Weddin' anniversary and
you tell us she's there in the earth

before taking us boys out for a special dinner
and after maybe a movie like we do on our own
birthdays, so we'll always think of Momma

as always being with us? . . . How can she be away
taking care of a little boy who needs her more
than we do . . . and at the same time in this earth.

XXVII

—Already the tombstone Big Billy paid for up front
when Momma died is crumbling from neglect—
it used to irritate him to see his name

carved in it deep beside hers with the date of
his birth, blank, the date of his mortality (how
many times must he play with the date,

fill it in with despair!?) Big Billy never missing
Friday night Benediction and Stations Of The Cross once and
always going to early, early Mass,

Five O'Clock Mass, his whole individuality
given up to a warm sensual fright love of God
in terror of His striking him dead . . .

XXVIII

Big Billy lies buried now in Thomaston, Maine, of
the clear blue lobster-water country, beside our mother
who was crumbled dust before I was a grown man.

But she gave me myself and now I give myself to her.
How come in my secret head I'm thinking
all the time what I was told on a Christmas eve

when I was seven, that Mamma just went to be with
a little boy who needed her more than
I did, than me and Young Billy did, but, as

if that was never said never told me, by the
time I'm ten years old we go with Big Billy
not batting an eye out to the old meadow

the community put its dead into forever
and God help me if I'd ever bring it up
but my heart wanted to believe my Mamma'd

come back to me . . . but don't ever dare
bring it up to Big Billy, how can she be in
this earth you keep bringing us to and

away taking care of another little boy who
needed her more than I did, we did? Oh
I wanted her to be with

that other boy and maybe
maybe coming back sometime
then in this earth.

XXIX

A drop of testicle juice hit her egg
and here I am in love with her.
We never knew each other as adults

but I am, finally, what she made me,
cuddling me in her arms and walking
me when I was puny sick and all

the while whispering to me that she
loved me and if there was another
boy she went to who needed her

more than I did she never once
ever loved him like she loved my
brother Young Billy and me . . .

not for a split instant . . . so all you
grown-ups who didn't know how to
just let me share my grief in her dying

I rise above you, whatever you ever did to me,
I am put together again hard, I will break
no further, I have become me.

> Down down deep in the sea
> th'lobster wait for
> Father's Lahty . . .

XXX

> "Mr. Dock," accordion
> jello face snapped Boppledock
> back . . . "They're
>
> here to lift you to hospital."
> Weakly, very tired, Boppledock
> wearily nodded . . .

"Hey, pal . . . you all right!?"
"Am I all right!! Wha-choo
talkin' 'bout?" Bop laughed . . .

. . . "Know what, Sergeant . . . I mean
Master Sergeant Alfred Kelly!?"
Accordion jello face dropped easily

to his haunches again beside
Bop like he'd pulled this kind
of duty since the beginning of time . . .

"What's funny, old fella?" Bop
looked up . . . the young guerrilla who
had pointed the automatic

at him when there was a threat
he would shake up life, had
appeared and stood now by

accordion jello face. Bop shook his head to
clear his vision, just for a split instant
accordion jello face's

features seemed to change
like seeing a skull through an X ray.
"Tell me somethin' " Bop seemed

almost shy . . . "I all of a sudden sure
don't feel like fightin' f'much." He
looked very hard at accordion

jello face. "I guess you don't
see what I mean" . . . the young
guerrilla reached a pack of

cigarettes over to Bop . . . "No, they're
death!" Bop shuddered. Master Sergeant
Kelly looked at the young guerrilla

like a boss at a subordinate. "I see
what you mean." Accordion
jello face whispered.

"Y'know," Bop went on as if
he hadn't heard him . . . "Kelly, d'you know
if you could ever git to th'point

where you can do somethin'
with no profit in it f'you . . ."
Accordion jello face's head was nodding.

A breeze blew the birthday candles out of
Bop's eyes . . . The old Victrola
was broken and the needle of Bop going

aimlessly all over the record . . . Accordion
jello face stood up. It was apparent
he was no longer needed . . .

. . . "Don't worry,"
he said grinning . . .
"The world won't end, it's too expensive!"

Lying on the stretcher Bop watched
the young guerrilla holding a piece of
polished tin he was using as a mirror

slanting bright bright sun at Bop as he was
entranced with the joy of his young image.
Bop's eyes winced shut against that

bright flash imprinted on his lids, dark
boxes vibrating like heartbeats
trying to thrust through and floating

through Bop's thoughts; I've progressed
in th'possibility of annihilation with
th'knowledge that like a young guerrilla

controlling th'sun in a piece of tin
we all must see to it th'sun doesn't
get away from us . . . Bop thought now

of Mercutio's wound, a strange gladness in
the remembrance. He hugged these thoughts
like a fine companion met again

in this new place. Feeling himself
lifted now, Bop
closed his eyes.

Earliest Poems:
Poetic Thoughts, 1944

Someday I'll Be Dead

Someday I'll be dead
and all of you will mourn,
not because I'm dead
because another one of you is gone.

You'll be thinking of your turn
just around the bend
where bowed beneath your Maker's feet
you will meet your end.

Someday I'll be gone
and you will have my cares
like puppets on a string dancing
up on makeshift airs
you'll wonder when your turn will come.

We're quite a marionette
a show for all to see
and when I'm dead and gone
you'll remember me.

Not as one you loved or knew,
as one you needed to get
your performance through.

The Leaf

I hang upon a tree in Spring
my beauty glowing bright.
Through Summer until early Fall
I never think of flight.
But as days wear on and on
I'm bored and yearn to fly.
So don't be scared if as you walk
you see a leaf go by.

I spin, turn in splendor true
and somersaults I do.
As I go I wonder why
I cannot start anew, once more
to hang in beauty's eyes
a young, fragrant leaf.
To think that I've grown old and gray
is hardly my belief.

Some people think me burned in fire
or dust in slow decay.
When all the while I'm in the trees
from which I'll bud next May.

JULY 1989